SLEEPING WITH DOGS

Sleeping with Dogs

a peripheral autobiography

BRIAN SEWELL

QUARTET

First published in 2013 by
Quartet Books Limited
A member of the Namara Group
27 Goodge Street, London W1T 2LD

A catalogue record for this book
is available from the British Library

ISBN 978 0 7043 7325 9

Typeset by Antony Gray
Printed and bound in Great Britain by
T J International Ltd, Padstow, Cornwall

Contents

For Dean Marsh,
who assisted at the obsequies of
Nusch, Jack and Winckelmann,
and who will bury me and Lottie.

Acknowledgements

When I began to write this book about my dogs, there were in the manuscript occasional references to 'the vet', but as my life wore on and the animals in it grew in number, so did the interventions of 'the vet' and I realised how great a part these saintly men had played in all our lives. They cured the ills, gave me peace of mind, perfectly understood the complex and deep nature of the bond between man and dog, and deserved better than the cool anonymity of 'the vet'. The name of one I cannot recall and did not meet – he saw to Penny in her last late months in Castle Hedingham, and was more interested in cattle than small dogs; and the name of another, in Wimbledon when I was newly there, I do not care to mention, for it was his cruel incompetence that compelled me to take my later dogs back to the surgery in Kensington, of which I had been a client for some forty years.

This veterinary surgery in Earl's Court Road had several incarnations – as Sinclair and Williams, Williams and Balmer, and as the Abingdon Veterinary Surgery with Russell Williams as its first linchpin. He, familiarly known as Rusty, was very tall, slim and, eventually, bent of back from stooping over operating tables – and it was the bent back that drove him into retirement. In emergencies a telephone call to his home was never rebuked, and his wife willingly tolerated a house full of broken animals. Reginald Balmer, in stockiness a physical contrast, was invariably as kind, if not for so long. When Onno Wieringa, a jolly Dutchman, took over, he too

9

looked after my dogs with astonishing intuition, great kindness and deft expertise. More recently, in Wimbledon, Roger Bralow has understood me as much as the ailments of my animals, recognising that what I have most wanted is tenderness for them and the brutal truth for me. I owe all these vets a great debt for their professional humanity and Franciscan benevolence.

I must also express my gratitude to photographers, professional, amateur and largely forgotten, who have provided the illustrations for this book. Of Prince, the dog of my pre-war penniless infancy, I have only memory. Given at sixteen or so a second-hand Kodak Brownie of ancient vintage, I swiftly learned to loathe all cameras and have never developed the customs and practices of photography; I am thus responsible only for the mostly blurred images of Penny, all that I have of her. Susie, Ginny and Spinoza sat for John Vere Brown, a portrait photographer (and painter) once much esteemed but now forgotten, long a close friend. Nicholas Vilag, a photographer for *Picture Post* in the Thirties and, after the war, an art dealer and another close friend, once walked with me in Kensington Gardens, I with my dogs, he with his camera, his shots, alas, too much about me. When Notoriety attached herself to me all sorts of professional photographers took pictures of my dogs as my accoutrements, and to these, particularly, I am grateful, yet owe apology, for having casually put their offerings in a big box marked DOGS, I now do not know who took which or when – and most of my attempts to trace and identify them have proved hopeless.

Prelude

Old habits die hard. Bedrooms in my boyhood were chill places, heated only at times of illness and grudgingly even then; beds were chill too, with heavy sheets of ancient inherited linen icy against the skin and woollen blankets so weighty that my small body was pressed into the mattress. In winter there was no such thing as falling asleep the moment one's head touched the pillow, for the first five minutes between the sheets were spent shivering and shuddering with cold as they sapped the heat from one's body – unless one had a dog.

Prince, before the war, slept on my bed. Penny, in the bitter winters of the later Forties, slept in it, radiating the igloo, as it were, and cuddling her meant that my front was warm as toast, no matter how clammy cold my back and far off feet might be. Susie slept both on and in my bed when I was seriously ill, judging my temperature, pressing against me to absorb the pain. I have ever since slept with all my dogs, one, two, three, or four at a time, waking, as I always do, with the not-quite dawn, but often making no attempt to leave my bed, so luxuriously seductive is the warmth on all sides. For an hour and more I have lain in this cocoon at least ten thousand times, ignoring the insistent thoughts of coffee and the working day, mindlessly drifting in and out of sleep, as immobilised by my companions as by anaesthesia. This, when the time comes, is how I wish to die.

☙ 1 ❧

Prince

How tall is a boy of three who at fifteen is fully grown at five feet and eight inches? The answer is more or less the height of Prince, the dog who came into my life on St Swithin's Day or thenabouts, my birthday (Rembrandt's too), in 1934. He was tall enough for me, standing, to put my arm about his neck as though we were equals, and reaching on his hind legs he was much the same height as my mother. Five years on, at the point of our parting, I had grown sufficiently to walk with my hand on his collar, an intense but simple pleasure. He was white, with black ears flopping, his long tail not docked but whipping me when wagging, pointerish, perhaps even a proper pointer – but how can I tell now, when then I was a child and a child's memory is all that I have of him?

I cannot recall his coming and played no part in it; fully grown, perhaps a year old, or two, no pet shop had him in the window; no neighbour, wearied by his turbulent antics, passed him on to us; no passing gypsy offered him. On Thursday, so to speak, there was no Prince, but on Friday he was the third part of our family. Did my mother find him wandering collarless and bewildered? Did he come whimpering to the door and beg to be let in? We were in Whitstable, in Ocean Cottage, a tiny primitive hideaway where I may well have been conceived, for my philandering father had taken a long lease on it to lend privacy to his affair with my mother; this was where we retreated when the after-effects of the Great Depression lay heavy on the lives of everyone and she could not afford the rent of even an attic in London. Whitstable was not then the fashionable resort that it now is; it was a working village, an oyster fishery, the harbour for the local fishing fleet, and a refuge for the red-sailed barges that transported goods along the north Kent coast. No one asked questions. No one knew that my mother had no husband and that I was illegitimate.

Why then, when we had not even tuppence to rub together for ourselves, did my mother add to our household a carnivorous animal that would need to eat as much as we? But add him she did, and he learned to leap through the rear window that was my tumbling access to the shingle beach, and became my playmate there, boisterous enough to knock me down, standing over me (mostly laughing) when felled, licking my face in affectionate apology, or dashing into the sea to retrieve great parcels of weed to be presented as a gift. He was my watchdog too, and on evenings when we were alone – my mother leaving the cottage for purposes mysterious – Prince lay watchful next to me, his head on my body, his eyes on the door.

I recall only one misdemeanour: a neighbour accustomed to hanging her Monday laundry on a line across the upper beach, came running – 'Come and see what your dog's done . . .' – and back we ran with her. Prince had pulled most of it from the line, more or less unharmed, but in attacking some vast undergarment of the combination kind (combinations combined vest and pants in one, had flies both front and rear kept closed by a hundred buttons, and were rarely sloughed in winter), he had caught his head in it and was leaping up and down half hanged and unable to detach himself.

Prince

What more can I say of Prince? I walked with him to neighbouring Tankerton and Seasalter – small achievements now that I look at a map, but adventures equal to Amboyna and the Amazon to a small boy. On our returns to the attics of Kensington I dare say he made finding lodgings difficult, but of this I was never aware, and in Kensington Gardens he could pretend to be the most mannerly of dogs. When I asked why my mother had called him 'Prince', she told me that she thought him handsome enough to have come from Schönbrunn Palace in Vienna where the Emperor of Austria kept his hunting hounds in luxury.

Insofar as a child is capable of love, I loved Prince. I did not know how much I loved him until the day of our sudden parting. Ours had for five years been an unquestioning companionship, an always-thereness, and I had no need to think about this brotherhood until too late. On the last day of August 1939, three days before the outbreak of World War II, Robert Sewell, the man who was to become my adoptive stepfather, drove to Ocean Cottage, expressed his conviction as a soldier who had fought throughout the 1914–1918 war that Whitstable would inevitably become a war zone and, watched by Prince, packed us and our baggage into the car. When all this was done, the doors of the cottage locked and bolted, the windows secured, he took Prince by the collar to the beach and shot him with a revolver that he had retained since 1918. I saw neither the revolver nor the deed, but I heard the shot and Robert's return without my dog required no questioning from me. He was, of course, quite right; Whitstable was, for much of the war, out of bounds, and London during the Blitz would have been no place for a dog – and on what, our rations near starvation level, could we have fed him? I might even argue that Robert's no nonsense, no argument, no tears, no pleading decisiveness in the matter was the cleanest way of dealing with it – but it was my first experience of emotional steel on my part, of silent unremitting hatred, of a determination not to let a powerful adversary know how hurt I was. Throughout the war, whenever he asked what I would like for Christmas or a birthday, I answered that I wanted nothing but a dog; worn down by this his response became customary – 'You can have a dog when the war is over,' and as though that settled the matter, asked again, 'Now, what do you want for Christmas?'

~~~ **2** ~~~

Penny

It was on 8 May 1945 that World War II drew to its close in Europe. Jubilant Londoners celebrated in the streets, gathered before Buckingham Palace, and danced the night away in Piccadilly, Soho and Trafalgar Square. For a day, boys at my school were allowed to join in, but I mounted my bicycle and pedalled all the way to Finchley to see a spotty and unlovable boy named Lacey (in those days we knew each other only by surname) whom I knew to have a litter of puppies. Long weeks earlier he educated us with descriptions of the mating of his little mongrel bitch, and we had had many bulletins since. I had five shillings in my pocket and hoped for change, but the uncomely Lacey argued that as I wanted the only bitch in the litter, he could not reduce the price; I could have a dog pup for three shillings and sixpence with eighteen pence in change, but the bitch was five bob or not at all.

I thought myself a fool for being so easily parted from my money when perhaps a better and cheaper puppy might be had elsewhere – but I had no idea where, my cycling the better part of twenty miles would have been for nothing and, most important, I would have lost the crucial point of holding my stepfather to his word on the very day the war was over, for I was certain that, with his customary parental duplicity, he would argue that the war was not over until the conflict with Japan was won, that rationing was far too punitive, that I was at a difficult stage at school (as, indeed, I was – but then all stages at school were difficult), or offer some other impeccably reasonable excuse for going back on his word. My only way to win was, without warning or delay, to confront him with a dog and hold him to his much repeated promise.

The deal disagreeably done, I packed the puppy in my school satchel, slung it over my shoulder and pedalled home. There I unpacked her, put her on the floor, pressed the doorbell of the flat and waited, more than a little fearful. My stepfather opened the door with 'Oh God, you haven't lost your key, have you?' and noticed the puppy only when she waddled past his feet. 'You little bugger,' he then said (of me rather than the pup), and called my mother. Fifteen years later, on 27 June 1960, I buried her small body in the rose bank of my mother's garden in Castle Hedingham – and there her bones still lie, the only bones of all the dogs since Prince that are not still in my possession, buried, exhumed, and now re-buried in my garden, to be persuaders for me at St Peter's Gate.

Like Prince, she was white, with floppy black ears, most of her face black too, and on her flank she had a perfectly circular (though it did not remain so) black patch that led to my calling her Penny; unlike Prince, she was shaggy. Tiny enough when I got her to hold in my cupped hands, she was, as an adult, light enough to tuck under my arm; when, in the late Fifties, Tibetan terriers became a popular breed, she was occasionally mistaken for one though her legs were longer, and it was often tactful to agree rather than insist on her mongrel status – doggy people can, in some circum-stances, be absurdly bossy.

The termination of the war did not mean that the end of

food rationing was nigh – indeed within the victorious month of May 1945 there were severe cuts in the already meagre allocations of meat, butter, sugar and even lard with which to fry or roast; we were allowed enough corned beef to make a sandwich once a week, enough cheese to make a single Welsh Rarebit, as much raw meat as could be had for a shilling (two ounces, perhaps), one egg every two weeks, and so on. For Penny I begged what I could from the butcher and was mostly rewarded with a pennyworth of 'lights', the ghastly pink spongy masses that were the lungs of sheep or pigs, unfit for human consumption. In due course even bread was rationed; the National Loaf that was neither white nor brown and, stale within hours, was the only food that could be bought by children with a handful of loose coupons already cut from ration books, and these the bakers in haste let flutter to the floor where, using Penny as an excuse, I could duck below the counter and retrieve enough to buy as much again.

It was on bread that Penny grew, on potatoes, greens and gravy, on the scrapings from roasting tins and casseroles, on the odd mouthfuls of meat or fish that I could covertly pass to her, and on what unwanted fat or gristle I could persuade my schoolmates to surrender from the dreadful food provided by our school. The habits of a lifetime were thus formed; all my dogs have been given titbits from the table and to eat without their company is inconceivable; before the doggy-bag became a fashion item there was always cellophane or grease-proof paper in which to wrap scraps from restaurants; and after a journey I always return with the last airline meal or railway sandwich.

Three events I remember from Penny's puppyhood. I had taken her on far too long a walk in what was still wild country to the north of London and, returning by the Underground from its furthest overground reaches with her sleeping in my lap, she, without waking, emptied her bladder. It was my first lesson – if I needed one – that those who have dogs must not be squeamish, but must take in their stride their pets' unexpected voidings of food, faeces and urine. For so small a creature Penny's warm flood was of surprising volume; it soaked through the thin flannel of my trousers into my underpants and, feeling it seep further, I stood to let it run down my leg into my shoe rather than into the upholstery. I laughed – at least until I realised that to any onlooker not a witness to the event, the wet patch in the crutch of my trousers must seem my mishap, not my dog's. When first attempting to teach her to walk to heel off the lead, she dashed into the road to greet a dog on the other side, right in front of a bus, a 52 to Victoria Station; she was aware of it just in time to halt and cower blindly to the ground as it drove over her, safe between its wheels. Not quite the lesson that I planned, it was learned immediately. The third event was a grass seed in her ear, one of those wickedly spiky V-shaped seeds that abound in neglected grass in August; she shook her head repeatedly; then she began to whimper; I could see nothing but knew that something must be done, for I recalled the pain of a mastoid operation when I was a child. 'The dog is yours,' my parents said, 'you must feed her, train her and care for her; she is your responsibility.' How does a boy of fourteen, knowing nothing of animals, with no access to a telephone or a directory and pocket money of only five shillings a week, find a vet for the first time in his life? But find one I did, miles away near my school, his name McClure, and it was he who, within moments, used tweezers to remove the seed and kindly charged no fee. For several years, in gratitude, I sent him home-made Christmas cards.

In spite of meagre rations, Penny grew into a tough and busy little bitch, highly intelligent, with a human vocabulary of fifty words or so; it was impossible to discuss Poussin without her mistaking him for Puss with a mad rush to the window to bark at the supposed cat, and I am convinced that, seemingly asleep, she listened to our conversations ready to react to words she recognised, sometimes so oddly that we asked ourselves what on earth we had just said, then to find that walk, bath, bed, dinner, car, biscuit or the names of our neighbours had been part of the last sentence. Among the few dogs then in the neighbourhood she had a menacing enemy, Bella, a brawny Staffordshire bull terrier who had once caught her by the tail and bitten it through, leaving only a stump that had to be tidied and sutured by Mr McClure, undying rancour the consequence – whenever Bella came into sight I had to lift Penny, fearless and furious, hug her to my chest and turn away.

I walked many miles with her in those early years, often with a school friend, Malcolm Tomkins, a boy of precocious literary bent who preferred cats to dogs and Sterne to Galsworthy, *Tristram Shandy* (that great bore) in his view the greatest novel in the English language. We took Green Line buses out of London and walked cross-country to pick up others on which to return, having inspected some country house or other monument between, leaving a forlorn Penny tethered at the door. As many as fifteen miles we walked and Penny, darting hither and yon, perhaps twice that number, happy to snooze while we roamed Penshurst, Luton Hoo or Polesden Lacey. The Penshurst walk was on Monday 22 July 1946, a week after my fifteenth birthday, the day that Zionist terrorists bombed the King David Hotel in Jerusalem – 476 injured, 91 killed by the Irgun Zvai Leumi led by Menachem Begin, later Prime Minister of Israel. We had reached Sevenoaks late in the afternoon of a glorious summer day and saw the headlines of the *Evening Standard*, and I was shocked to the point of feeling physically sick.

Penny's company made bearable the oppressive closeness of family holidays in Devon and on the Isle of Wight until, at sixteen, I could break free of them and stay at home, enjoying an extraordinary sense of both liberty and responsibility while my parents were bickering in Brighton in an hotel they could barely afford. She sat with me if I chose to paint in the open air (at seventeen I thought myself another Monet), and she sometimes came to Mass, sitting unseen among the pads on which we knelt in some shadowed corner of the church. From the very beginning she slept with me, on the bed in summer, in it in winter, and when I joined the army for two years' National Service, she pined and my mother could only walk her on the lead, for if she saw a soldier in uniform – then a common sight – she ran to him, and some strange boy on thirty-six hours' leave, surprised but not displeased to be enthusiastically greeted, could not understand her sudden change in behaviour when voice and scent failed to match her expectation. That she could distinguish a soldier from a civilian suggests considerable intelligence.

Out of the army, I bought a car and observed on journeys regularly made – to an old friend in Saffron Walden, to my godmother in Worthing, to my mother who had removed to Castle Hedingham – that Penny swiftly settled and went to sleep, always to waken when we were only a mile or two from our destination; but on irregular journeys of much the same length and even, in part, on the same roads, she sat alert and watching. How could this be? How did she distinguish between one journey and another? For me it was the first proof of, in animals, a level of perception or intuition beyond the capacity of humans, of which some of my later dogs were to provide further evidence.

As a student at the Courtauld Institute I neglected her – the days were long, the studying intense, the absences abroad lasted for weeks and even months – and Penny became more my mother's dog than mine until I was offered a job at Christie's as an authority on old masters (now even I utter a hollow laugh) and found a flat in Phillimore Place, in Kensington, from which it was possible to walk to work through Kensington Gardens, Hyde Park and Green Park, taking Penny with me. At Christie's she sat at my feet, her snoozing interrupted by a lunchtime dash back to Green Park, but then the tireless Penny tired, something about her body language suggesting that she no longer relished the brisk morning walk and that at the end of the day she would rather go home by bus.

One wintry weekend early in 1960, we drove down to Castle Hedingham and I left her with my mother – 'Two old bitches keeping company,' she put it. All went quietly well until 26 June, when my mother telephoned to say that Penny was 'out of sorts, but perhaps it is only the heat'; I suggested that the vet should be consulted – not a man I much liked, more given to large agricultural animals and drily unsympathetic in his attitude to small dogs – and to the vet she went the following morning. He felt something not to his liking, suggested an exploratory investigation, explored, did not care for what he found and increased the anaesthetic to lethal level. 'Cancer,' he said to my mother, handing her the corpse to carry home, 'riddled with it.' That evening, speechless with grief, I drove the seventy miles to bury her. It was the day sometimes dedicated to the Seven Sleepers of Ephesus and their dog Kratim or Kratimer, one of only ten animals admitted to Muhammad's paradise.

≫ 3 ≪

Susannah, Susie

I grieved for Penny. I had, as it were, grown from boy to man with her, the years then so much longer than they seem when the graveyard beckons, learning the disciplines of ineluctable responsibility for a creature that must daily be fed, watered and exercised, learning something too of love and physicality, of the pleasures – indeed the values – of fondling and of falling asleep with her trusty little body in my bed. I was ten weeks short of fourteen when I bought her and two weeks short of twenty-nine when I buried her; she had been my closest companion for more than half my life and, never having questioned how close-bound we had become, I was quite unprepared for the emotional consequences of her death. She had never been my toy, nor had there been anything of the brotherliness of my relationship with Prince, nor did I ever think of her as an adopted child satisfying a frustrated parental urge; she was my dog and we were man and dog in a primeval bond, and that was that – though I believe that I was a kinder and more considerate boy for having her, and a more compassionate man.

I thought often of another dog, these thoughts engendering so sharp a grief that I did nothing for three months, and then did something quite by chance. It was a Saturday morning halfway through September 1960 and I was in Harrods, then a shop with gravitas, on some errand for my mother, to whose house in Hedingham I was to drive in time for tea.

On impulse, yet quite deliberately, for it was on an upper floor and not come upon by happenstance, I went to what they called their zoo – and a zoo it was, at least in the sense that it would supply a tiger cub were that what one wanted. There I saw a lean and leggy pup, her coat mid brown, short-haired and smooth, her nose, eyes and toenails brown to match, her tail undocked, her ears long and floppy. I thought she resembled an Hungarian pointer yet was sure that she was not, but there was neither price nor label on her cage. To my questions the answers were that she was three months old, her dam an Hungarian pointer, her sire a whippet and that both had pedigrees – as though that were of any consequence in an unplanned crossbreed – the price £5 (a Harrods price for a worthless puppy). I asked to see her walk: her back was straight, her legs long, her gait confidant. When I picked her up she sank her forepaw claws into my tie, an expensive thing of coarse woven silk in black and gold, and could not be detached; as with one exquisite thread drawn the tie would be ruined, there followed a pantomime in which the Harrods girl attempted to hold the pup still while I unhooked her claws. This mid-air operation failed; both warp and weft of the precious tie were ravaged (I have it still) and, having rummaged for a fiver in my pocket, I walked off with the pup still clinging to it.

In the garden at Hedingham she at once showed her paces as a running dog, leaping like an adult thoroughbred over Penny's grave in the rose bank that divided the long slope into flat upper and lower lawns, and seeing resemblance to a girlfriend whose long hair and coat tails seemed always to stream in the wind as she ran for buses in Kensington High Street, I named her Susannah; inevitably Susannah became Susie. Her official birthday was proclaimed to be 17 June, a day dedicated to St Moling, an Irish hermit saint who kept a pet fox for company. I prepared a box for her bed, within reach should she whimper in the night, and with some persuasion she seemed settled in it, but the moment I got into my bed she bounded onto it. For an age we fought this on-off tussle, and then, as I got into my bed for the umpteenth time, slumping onto my back as I pulled the blankets over me, she seized the moment and with perfect timing and perfect aim sprang from her box and, diving through the fly of my pyjama trousers, scrabbled down the left leg until, jammed against my thigh, she could go no further. I could get no safe purchase to pull her back, the claws that had ruined my tie were now embedded in me, and I was helpless with laughter. I undid the cord, pulled down the trousers, recovered her and went to sleep with her in my arms. In doing so I discovered how warm a smooth-coated dog is. If I knew Prince to exude warmth, I had forgotten, for he was long ago and I only a child. It is not that Penny had been a cold dog, but her coat was shaggy and insulating, and, cool to the touch when snuggling against my tummy, it was I who gave her my warmth long before she gave me hers. Susie, smooth as silk, was immediately warm to the touch and infinitely more comforting than any hot water bottle. In the whole of her long life she slept nowhere else.

The following day we had a small joint of beef for lunch. My mother's dining room opened off the kitchen and had probably been the servants' room, for its other door led to the back staircase. The beef was resting on the table and we were in the kitchen, Susie with us until she seemed suddenly to take flight like a guided missile and, sliding and slithering across the table, sending cutlery and glass in all directions, seizing the beef, she tore up the stairs. Dashing after her I was just in time to see her disappear down the front stairs – and so the game began, a mad scramble up one and down the other, round and round, to and fro, until I caught her with something like a rugger tackle. The joint recovered, I cut away the outer layers and, rather gingerly, we ate the inner core.

She was two or so before she outgrew her madcap adolescence and could be trusted not to tug at curtains until the poles in their brackets broke away from the walls, not to turn my bed into a bird's nest, not to chase sheep, horses and even trains along their tracks – all this was curiosity and *joie de vivre* rather than malign intent, but that is not quite how the Hedingham farmers saw it, nor the nose-in-the-air riders in Hyde Park. She was, in fact, highly intelligent and very easily trained; once rebuked, she rarely repeated a mis-demeanour, but the misdemeanour had first to be performed before she understood that it was forbidden. Half a century ago it was possible to walk a dog off the lead in the streets of London, to train her to step into the gutter to empty her bowels, to respond to the word 'stay' by immediately staying exactly where she was, and to 'over' by crossing the road precisely at my pace and below whichever happened to be my free hand. As parked cars were then comparatively few, the Porsche very rare, the Ferrari quite unknown, most British cars overweight and underpowered, buses hardly ever exceeded the pace of a running man and cyclists sat upright on machines equipped with bells, the street was far safer territory then. It was even safe to park my old Daimler drop-head coupé with the hood down, leaving Susie at the wheel.

That she adored the Daimler was clear from her choosing to sit in it alone when it was parked in my mother's garden and I was mowing the grass or pruning raspberry canes. It had a bench front seat and, on the move, she leaned against me and watched the world go by – she was not a dog for leaning into the wind and barking; nor was she, like Penny, a dog who slept in familiar territory; she was, as it were, an intelligent and observant companion. Antoine Seilern, passionate connoisseur and collector and the most generous of donors to the Courtauld Institute, used to drive into London from his Buckinghamshire farm with a pet pig in the passenger seat beside him – a pink pig as perfectly well-behaved as Susie; years later, on discovering a small sketch in oils of very much the same pink pig, by Arthur Lemon (who became a pupil of Carolus-Duran after working for a decade as a cowboy in California), I bought it and, in an act of foolish sentiment, presented it to Susie who, in later middle age, lost her lissome figure, became plump, and was occasionally called Piggie. She showed not the slightest interest in the painting but I still think of it as hers.

When she was a year old, in 1961, I spent a week on Dartmoor with a friend who wished to paint a landscape there. It was to be Susie's first experience of the all-day walk of twenty miles without a halt. It was also her first encounter with water – we came upon a leat, an open water-conduit, and into it she leaped with a great splash, and under. She scrambled out, shook herself, and stood looking at it as though considering some deep philosophical problem; and then, with the delicacy of a lady not wanting to get her hair wet, plopped gently back into the leat and let it waft her along in its slow current, adjusting her course with an occasional dog-paddle.

Coming upon the ring of standing stones known as Grey Wethers, just below Sittaford Tor, she sensed some presence that disturbed her, or perhaps even saw a ghost. I did not much care for the bleak atmosphere myself – and I have never cared for its big brother, Stonehenge, a disappointing mystery – but I could neither sense nor see a reason for Susie's risen hackles, her sudden flight and her refusal to slow down as, shouting, I sped after her. She stopped only when she blundered into a bog. Nine years later, in the autumn of 1972, when we moved into 19 Eldon Road in middle Kensington, she again sensed something, this time on the stairs to the kitchen and, unable to run, simply lowered her haunches, trembled, raised her hackles and howled. This she did too often to ignore; besides, I too sensed something disagreeable – a chill and a stench through which I could pass in a single stride, of much the same height and volume as a human being; and it moved, as though coming to stand beside me at the kitchen sink or blocking my way on the stairs. One evening, again encountering it on the stairs, I sat and talked to it; I told it that I had no knowledge of its misery nor of its cause, that I had no means of remedying what had happened in the past nor did I want in any way to make it worse, and that I wanted only that the house should be a happy place for me and my dogs. Anyone witnessing this entirely one-sided conversation would have thought me mad, but, by coincidence no doubt, the column of cold and mortal stink disappeared and never again was Susie so disquieted.

At Christie's she behaved perfectly until early in June 1963. I was in the final stage of preparing a sale of paintings from the studio of Augustus John; they were the leftovers of a long lifetime, unfinished, neglected and filthy and had to be made presentable; all had been cleaned and stretched and a handful had to be framed, but there was so little time in hand that the framer had taken measurements and made the frames in his workshop concurrently with the restorer working on the canvases. A sensible framer would have added a margin of millimetres for error, for no canvas is ever a perfect rectangle – and of this, proof lay in one that was some two by three metres one way, but not the other.

The framer, chosen by the John family, was immensely fat, breathless and sweating, his hands unfittingly small and delicate, his fingers those of a child. He propped the canvas against a wall and tried the frame against it; it did not quite fit. He tried it the other way up; little more than a narrow strip or fillet (in French a baguette), it whipped and I thought would come apart at the corners; with my assistance we put the canvas flat on the floor, face up, placed the frame on it and tried to force it on. All the while Susie had been motionless under my desk, but when the framer, his back to her, stooped, wheezing, to put all his weight on the frame, faced by the vast bulk of his bottom, she sprang into action and sank her teeth into one enormous spreading buttock. He tipped forward onto the canvas, the frame broke apart at the lower right-hand corner, and Susie returned to the shadow of my desk to lie there as though nothing had happened. The painting was sold without a frame.

All those years ago the old wives' anthropomorphic belief was that every bitch should have at least one litter if she is to be sweet-tempered in old age and free of gynaecological problems. Unwillingly I consented. My mother wanted a bitch of her own, the friend with whom I had been to Dartmoor wanted another, and it was he who found George, a whippet notorious for entering Underground tunnels at Edgware Road station, near his home, and bringing the northern reaches of the District Line to a halt; George's mistress too wanted a pup. When Susie showed signs of coming into season at the end of March 1964, my mother reckoned that 2 April might be the best day for what she insisted on calling 'the wedding', and so George and his entourage were driven to Hedingham and let loose on the lawn. My mother was right about the date, but the business that followed seemed ludicrous, perfunctory and punishing.

When it was evident that Susie was pregnant – though she kept her figure well enough to make us think that the litter would be small – I left her with my mother to deal with diet, exercise and nursing matters. Over the weekend of 5 June, without the least fuss, delivery began – a pair of pups and then a second pair; for three hours she licked and nuzzled them and we concluded that there would be no more, for she then, minutes before midnight, went into the garden to empty her bladder and returned to ask for food. I fed her and went to bed. At three in the morning I went down to see her – she had chosen to roost under the dining room table – and found six puppies; at breakfast there were eight. George may have seemed perfunctory but he had well and truly done his duty. 'Bloody hell,' I thought, 'we are certain of homes for only three.'

Susie was the perfect mother – eight equal puppies and no runt. At five weeks or so a friend offered my mother a holiday in his house in Winchelsea, very near the sea, the garden surrounded by a high wall, a daily woman to do all the chores. 'Bring Susie and the pups,' he said. Years before, as a schoolboy spending a summer vacation working with pups belonging to the Greyhound Racing Association, I had been trained to settle their stomachs before they travelled by breaking a raw egg into their open jaws – one gulp and it has gone and they will not be sick. It was a fine day and we set off with the car's hood down, Susie and all eight pups on the bench seat between us. Within five miles, up came the eggs, most of them into my lap. I stopped the car and, as I got out, the eggs slithered down my trousers to the ground. A few miles more and there was proper vomit; and after more miles still, travellers on the ferry across the Thames at Woolwich recoiled when rash enough to peer into the car. At Winchelsea every shred of my clothing went straight into the washing machine. And at Winchelsea we were offered homes for three of the pups. My mother chose to keep the most whippety of them, an almost ethereal bitch the colour of pine wood newly cut, and called her Ginevra, after the earliest portrait by Leonardo da Vinci, a moon-face girl to whom she bore no resemblance.

The old wives' tale about the gynaecological well-being of bitches turned out not to be true. Five years on, when she was nearly nine, I left Susie with my mother and made one of my many journeys to New York. I was still dazed with jet lag when the telephone call came. Susie, my mother said, was desperately ill, hysterectomy essential if she was not to die. I returned to London on the first available plane, in time to take her to Rusty Williams and hold her hand, as it were, while she slipped into unconsciousness – an act my mother was to hold against me when she in turn fell ill when I was again in America and I stayed where I was. I made amends on my return and sent her to George Pinker, one of the Queen's surgeons (at vast expense), but for ever after, at the mere sniff of a cold, she reproached me with 'You came back for your dog, but refused to come back for me.'

Susie's surgery done, she recovered with astonishing speed, but there was a new anxiety about her behaviour, as though she did not want to lose sight of me and needed constant reassurance with a touching hand. When Peter Langan, the restaurateur (and close friend) invited me to dinner at Odin's, I refused on the grounds that it was too soon to leave Susie alone in the house – 'Bring her,' he said, and so, while we ate the experimental new dishes that he had devised, she sat on a chair next to me with a dish of very lightly browned diced steak before her on the table. Picking each dice separately and toying with it with extraordinary delicacy for a human being, let alone a dog, looking about her between morsels, she played her part perfectly. 'Christ Almighty,' said an Australian at a table across the aisle, 'now I've seen everything. Fucking dogs eat at this restaurant.' 'I own this joint,' said Peter with a menacing scowl, 'and I'd rather have a dog at my table than any fucking digger.'

Half a century ago, over a period of years, I was repeatedly laid low with bouts of jaundice, first contracted while working in Germany. With one particularly bad bout, yellow as stale mustard, I took to my bed, and so did Susie. For weeks she lay beside me, not with her usual rumbustious enthusiasm, but with utmost care, gently easing her body against mine as though seeking as much contact as possible without causing me the slightest discomfort – with jaundice at its height the patient aches in every bone and muscle. Again and again it seemed to me that she sensed when I was most in pain, and in discreetly pressing her back against the length of mine, sought to absorb it from me whenever I groaned. It was my first experience of a dog's intuitive understanding of illness in a human being. When I recovered, her careless jubilance returned, but this illness had been a turning-point of sorts, for she became my guardian, protecting me from visitors. We were inseparable.

Occasionally, I suppose for old times' sake and sentiments,

she and I walked without the other dogs, making the point that she was privileged as dowager. It was on one of these slow ambles on a summer evening that Susie showed a sign of intelligent awareness extraordinary in a dog. Daimlers, proper Daimlers (that is nobly large cars with fluid flywheels and epicyclic gears), had by then long since died away and I had taken to driving a maroon Peugeot 404, a very sensible but common car, two-a-penny on the streets of London. On this particular evening mine was parked a block away to the north, but we walked south into the garden square of Cornwall Gardens where there are great trees and little traffic, and an old dog can safely take her time over interesting smells. We passed a maroon Peugeot identical to mine and she paused expectantly. I walked on; she stayed put. I had to go back and put her on the lead to make her move, grudgingly, looking back over her shoulder. We had passed two other examples of the Peugeot 404, one silver, the other navy blue, and she had ignored them, but the maroon car, to which she cannot have been drawn by (literally) familiar smells, and which was distinguished only by its colour, she clearly identified as mine (or hers). If, as I understand from far more learned dogologists than I, dogs cannot see colour, can they instead discern the subtle distinctions of tone to which colour is reduced with glaucous vision? – very subtle indeed when maroon and navy blue are reduced to shades of grey. She must also have identified the shape.

In due course Susie went blind – a slow business in which touch became our common language – even more so when deafness followed. With the loss of these senses she became an obstinate and contrary old girl and insisted, come what may, on certain rituals on the morning walk, leaving a trace of urine at the base of particular trees, disturbing the Canada geese cropping the grass near the Round Pond and taking a dip if she felt inclined, and snuffling round the Serpentine Gallery. These unbreakable customs were a reassurance to us both, but occasionally one of her granddaughters, Schubert, grew impatient with her dawdling and took to shouldering her away from her obsessions and steering her back to the pack; in the end, if I too lost patience, I could say to Schubert 'Go and get Susie,' and she would.

On her last Christmas Day I took all the dogs to Wimbledon Common because snow had fallen and I thought a little comparatively rough country and a pot-pourri of strange smells would give them the sort of intellectual pleasure that reading a different newspaper gives to me. When we scrambled down to the Leg-of-Mutton Pond it was frozen. If a blind dog can smell the difference between ice and water, then Susie's nose betrayed her; not hearing my shout, she dropped onto the ice, broke through it and broke more as, in evident alarm, she frantically dog-paddled, but away from the bank. I had no option but to haul off as much of my clothing as I could in two seconds and go after her. I knew the water to be only four feet deep or so, but in the icy cold it was a hell of a shock. I grabbed her collar, turned her round, steered her to the bank and tried to push her out, but with my feet on the soft muddy bottom, the added height of the bank meant that my nose was at ground level and, frozen to the bone, found that I had neither the strength to push Susie up those extra inches, nor find the purchase to heave myself out of the water. It seemed an age before any of the several spectators crouched to offer a hand. Then I was more than glad that I had shed my duffel coat, sweater and shirt (had I not, getting out would have been even more difficult) for I had things with which to get the worst of the wet from Susie's coat and the duffel to give me some warmth.

The last six months of her life she was a contented old thing, happy even to enjoy a gentle wrestling match with all the sham snarling and biting of such play, rolling belly-up in mock surrender, but on 15 August 1975, two months after her sixteenth birthday, she barked in the night and would not be comforted. In the morning it was clear that she was unwell. Within twenty-four hours I was due to leave for Turkey for six weeks or so and, as there were still preparations to be done, it was with some impatience that I took her to Rusty Williams, and left her there. The day spent on those preparations, I returned home to find a message from him: Susie had died – died after sharing my bed for all those years, died on an operating table among unfamiliar smells and in the hands of strangers. I vowed then that never again would any dog of mine – if it were possible – die without my presence.

Brown coat, brown eyes, brown nose, brown toenails – I collected her limp body and drove to Winchelsea to bury her in the garden there where she had spent so many days. Years later, when that house was sold to strangers, I dug up her bones and brought them to London in a box; years later still I buried them again, under a sapling oak in the garden of the house in Wimbledon where I now live.

My grief for Susie had to be contained; leaving for Turkey the following morning immediately cut it short, but the intensity of the loss prompted sudden recollections that for months caught me unawares with a welling tear and a catch in my throat. Moreover, to drive to Turkey was to encounter a thousand dogs, starving, limping, dead, every one of them the trigger to a memory. These were not in Germany and

Austria, nor even in the length of what for half a century was Jugoslavia, but on crossing the border into Greece they were everywhere, single and in packs, dead and bloated by the road or running for their lives, a handful – inexperienced – hoping for man's charity. In Greece it seems that drivers deliberately go out of their way to run down dogs as though to do so is a national necessity; many are killed outright, others, with broken backs and legs, are left to die in agony. In Turkey drivers do not give a dog the moment of deceleration that will save its life, but nor do they accelerate or deviate – as do the Greeks – to maim or slaughter it; once, in Ramadan, the month of fasting, I witnessed the driver asleep at the wheel of a lorry plough into and through a flock of sheep, killing most of them and the shepherd's dog, though not the shepherd. It was an appalling, bloody sight, but, for the sheep a kinder sudden death than the Islamic slaughter of the abattoir whither the shepherd was driving them.

4

Ginevra, Ginny

Susie's was not the first burial in that Winchelsea garden, nor the only exhumation. Her daughter – at first essentially my mother's dog, but later as much mine when, increasingly frail, my mother came to live with me – had died earlier in 1975, on 20 March, at ten past three in the afternoon, to be precise. This is the day dedicated to St Cuthbert, a saint whose bones, anticipating Ginnie's, were exhumed and much translated. Poor Ginevra; Susie's pup from the litter of 1964, sleek and slim, delicate and diaphanous against the light, her smooth coat the faintest beige paling to white ash on cheeks and belly, her eyes dramatically large and dark, altogether more whippety than many whippets of long pedigree, she was oppressed by her mother's dominance, cowed by her top-doggery – never, even long after she was both deaf and blind, was a bitch more tyrannical than Susie with her pretty daughter. Like so many spinster daughters, Ginny was attendant on her mother – but a spinster she was not.

In spite of the contrary evidence in Susie's case that, to prevent 'women's troubles in later life', every bitch should have at least one litter, my mother plotted to continue Susie's line by finding a mate for Ginny. I argued strenuously against it; I did not believe the old wives' nonsense and I had had much experience of my mother's misbegotten schemes supposedly for my benefit. If and when Susie departed this life I intended to find, not her duplicate, but a dog as different as possible, an Alsatian perhaps, and find her myself.

My mother would not be baulked. She had, walking Ginny, occasionally encountered a certain Colonel Kirby with a handsome dog called Samson, who was nothing in particular but might, from a distance, be taken for a skinny Labrador. Colonel Kirby foolishly opined that the experience of mating might be as good for Samson as for Ginny (though I detected, I thought, a disconcertingly personal glint in his eye, as though in recollection of things long past) and, with my mother, conspired to bring it about. On 22 June 1970 these two old people put their dogs together and watched them conjugate. What, I wondered, went through their minds as spectators of this gross activity? Now that I am into my eighties, I think I know.

Susie had carried her eight pups very tidily; Ginny, fine-boned and slender, was not at ease with hers and they hung low in her stretched belly. I feared that Samson's spawnings might be too large and kill her and Rusty was reassuring only in his promise to come if we called him, be it day or night. And night it was, of course, and on my mother's bed. She called me shortly before midnight and I dashed upstairs to find Ginny in evident distress, one small hind leg protruding from her. Gently I pushed it back and, astonished that such a delicate frame could support so large an aperture, attempted with my fingers in her to turn the pup about and bring it out head first. And so I did, but it was dead, a beautiful dog pup, inert and unresponsive to Ginny's feeble licking and my hapless pinching its rib cage in the hope of breath. The second pup emerged head first more easily, but was still attached by the cord when, not Rusty but Reg Balmer, rang the front doorbell; Ginny responded as she always did – she leaped from the bed and tore downstairs barking, the pup bouncing after her, bump, bump, bump, the cord unbroken. Thick carpeting saved her; to my surprise the little creature, still largely parcelled in her membrane, survived this *post partum* trauma and grew into a handsome bitch. Over the next four hours, four more puppies were born without incident.

Susie played no part, not even as spectator, in all this, but the following day made it evident that she was not best pleased and, making deadly intentions clear, had to be prevented from approaching the nursery. Ginny had never quarrelled with her mother but from the day the pups were born became hysterically anxious if she sensed the old bitch nearby. The murderous menace diminished only when the pups were weaned and began to understand the hierarchy of which they were only the lowest rung. The largest by far, a black dog – Colonel Kirby having decided that one dog was enough and declined his customary right to first choice from the litter – was taken by an old friend from my years at Christie's, whose ancient Alsatian had just died, and christened George; his brother, Hector, went to the niece of one of my old art history professors, Tom Boase, and went to live in very grand quarters in The Little Boltons; but no one at all was interested in the three bitches. My mother adopted one, a brindle of occasionally evil temper, and called her Spinoza – a name that was never shortened; the other two fell to me – the beautiful leggy blonde pup who had bounced down the stairs within moments of her birth, the fair Schubert, and the black runt, the only one with short legs and a barrel body with not a hint of whippet about her, and unkindly called Gamage, after a shop in Holborn famous for selling factory rejects and other imperfect goods.

Poor Ginny. Perhaps every sentence that I write about

her should begin with 'Poor Ginny' – certainly all my recollections of her begin and end with this lament. Sweet in temper, with a whippet's inclination to curl up somewhere warm and never be a nuisance, devoted to my mother yet demanding nothing of her, she should have been an only dog, not Susie's underling, not the guiding parent of a boisterous family. She was not built for pregnancy and it exhausted her. She educated the pups into their adolescence, but that done, never again did she run for the sheer joy of it, never again did she chase pigeons, squirrels and rabbits, and always close at heel, she was the one dog who could be trusted to walk the streets without a lead, but she was old before her time. Perhaps, at six, her first and only litter was too late; certainly – I am convinced – Samson was too big a mate for her.

Eventually she became pernickety about food. All the others would eat anything offered, but lived largely on jugged hare supplied by Peter Langan, one of whose constants in the restaurant was hare pâté, made only with the saddle, the rest extravagantly discarded and sent to me in a taxi with any other odds and ends that were otherwise destined for the bin. From such rich food Ginny turned away, at last settling on a diet of poached lambs' tongues – how medieval, I thought, just the sort of thing that might be recorded of Berengaria of Navarre or Isabelle of Angoulème, at the feet of whose tombstone effigies historic Ginnies lie. Early in 1974 it became obvious from her lethargy that something indefinable was amiss; Rusty diagnosed diabetes and from then on I had to inject a daily dose of insulin under the skin of her shoulder, after which she slept for an hour or so. It worked well at first; she regained energy and seemed as much as the others to relish the morning walk, but slowly the lethargy returned and she abandoned exercise. Within a year it seemed that the injected insulin had no effect; nor did any other stratagem proposed by Rusty, and in the afternoon on 20 March 1975, the day devoted to the patron saint of shepherds and their dogs (to swans and otters too), the much translated Cuthbert, lying on a favourite couch in the kitchen, she quietly faded away. With a spade in the boot of the car and Ginny's little body in a blanket next to me, I drove to Winchelsea, buried her and howled with grief, convinced that I had failed her.

The page for that day in my mother's diary is blank. She must, I think, have been so stricken by the death that she had no words for it; but on 20 March in every diary from 1976 to 1985 the death of 'my darling Ginny in 1975' is recalled. In 1986 the onslaught of dementia blanked the memory.

5

Hecate

Hecate, of all my dogs the only one to have a pedigree, was a whim, an impulse, a creature of my imagination, conceived in 1961, the year in which Ian Lowe, my assistant at Christie's, resigned, married Mary Howard and took to breeding whippets. 'If ever you have a perfect blue bitch pup,' I heard myself say, 'call her Hecate on her pedigree papers and let me have her.' Hecate, a mysterious deity of the ancient Greeks, eluding definition, simultaneously benign and terrible, protectress of hunters, herders and fishermen, warriors and athletes, yet queen of sorcery and mistress of the phantoms, ghosts and demons of the Underworld, howling hell-hounds her attendants, was to be mollified by sacrifices of honey, puppies and black female lambs left at every crossroad. Hers seemed a fine name for a bitch that would be invisible by night.

Ian was appointed assistant keeper at the Ashmolean Museum and, living in Oxforshire, almost slipped out of my life, our friendship reduced to rare encounters and the exchange of Christmas cards; Susie bore her litter, Ginevra became part of my life and the blue whippet pup was utterly forgotten until 9 August 1967, six years on, when I received a telegram: 'Hecate born yesterday. Delivery in three months.'

I had never seen a certificate of pedigree: she was registered as Nimrodel Hecate, after her dam, Nimrodel Belle Bleu (the daughter of another Nimrodel), her sire Stargazer, with dogs named Winged Foot, Black Brocade, Black Maria, Penelope, Samarkand and Fleeting This and That among her ancestors. On 24 October Mary and Ian brought me this piece of paper and a tiny, bright-eyed, perky little thing, tense and muscular to the touch, my fingertips sensing a faint tremor as though an electric current were conducted by her body; her coat, as fine and silken as a fieldmouse, would have made perfect eyebrows for a cosmeticked lady of the eighteenth century, a flawless dark steel grey that is, perversely, blue in pedigree parlance, with exactly matching claws. For a pup of ten weeks she was very small – small enough to be tucked into my pullover, peeping from its V-neck, supported by my left hand when we were on the move, but too small for any functional collar and far too small to risk her sleeping in my bed, though she evidently needed the warmth of another body to see her through the night.

Nor could that body be Susie's, for there was at once a significant problem – her menacing reaction. There was nothing of the tail-wagging curiosity of an older dog for a puppy, nothing of the mothering instinct that a pup's helplessness often rouses in a bitch; instead, Hecate's jaunty fearlessness engendered in Susie such evidently murderous intention that I could only foresee disaster. I could not leave them together – indeed they could not be in the same room even if I was with them, so furious was Susie's jealousy and so futile my attempts to soothe her. Of these attempts – embraces, cuddles, wrestlings, bribes – there were a thousand, but the jealousy never ceased to seethe and she was cunning in her attempts to outwit me. They could not be walked or fed together, I could not work at my desk unless one or

other was locked away, I could not go to a sale at Christie's
or Sotheby's without Hecate nestling in my jumper and, as
Susie had learned to operate door handles, locking her in
my bedroom was the preliminary to every ordinary action
of the day – cooking, showering, answering the door or
telephone – and this discipline became burdensome. In the
end Susie took to uncooperative sulking, refused food,
would not walk, would not respond when called, hid under
furniture in rooms that were rarely used and could never be
found when I had to leave the house.

Of all this, in late December, I bitterly complained to
John Vere Brown, the friend with whom Susie and I had
been to Dartmoor and who had procured George, the father
of her pups – of whom he had adopted one, only to lose her
to a passing car. 'I'll take Hecate if you like,' he said. 'Not,' I
replied, 'if you look after her as carelessly as you did Ginny's
sister.' Promises were made, solemn undertakings given,
and I let Hecate go. The effect on Susie was immediate –
the sulking ceased and at once she was again the warm
affectionate companion on my bed. I was miserable with
regret and cursed my weakness in having given in after only
two months, but I had had to surrender for Susie's sake.
John proudly registered his ownership of Hecate with The
Kennel Club.

In June 1968 notification of another change of ownership
reached The Kennel Club – back to me. On the eleventh of
that month I was on my way to The Pen Shop in Regent
Street, from which had come, even in my schooldays, all my
pens and their replacement nibs and bladders, when I saw,
perhaps fifty yards ahead, a blue whippet, off the lead. Then
she saw me, sprinted and leaped onto my shoulder (with
only a little scrabbling for the last few inches), ecstatically

licking my face. 'Bloody dog,' said John, catching up, 'she's never done that for me. You'd better have her back.' And so too, thought I, having seen her sans lead and collar ahead of him in busy Regent Street. It transpired that he had just left The Pen Shop and I thanked heaven for the coincidence.

At ten full months since her birth Hecate was as big as she would be, but that was more the size of an Italian greyhound than a fully grown whippet and my anxiety for her safety when we reached home was very great; Susie, however, showed no sign of animosity and welcomed her with the common activities of canine greeting. From this I concluded, not that in six months she had forgotten her jealousy (I don't think she ever forgot anything), but that her murderous instincts were directed only towards puppies, later, perhaps, confirmed by her response to Ginny's litter. The trio settled down in amity, Susie, by then a matronly eight, content to let Hecate snuggle against her on my bed, Ginevra at four still willing and eager to race about with Hecate and play all the whippet games, wonderfully fast and beautiful in movement.

At the nursing of Ginny's pups Hecate was a tolerated bystander, a maiden aunt of sorts occasionally shepherding a wanderer back to the nest or disdainfully clearing away a tiny turd. There was more shepherding to do in the garden – deliberately encouraged to become the haunt of birds and thus a tanglewood – and more still when we ventured on walks, for when the three remaining pups were half-grown, we could encounter no one without astonished enquiry (Hecate too, often mistaken for a pup), during which a wayward pup might wander off. 'What are their names?' everyone asked, and I grew weary of explaining Schubert, Gamage and Spinoza – of whom it seemed that no ordinary mortal had ever heard – why hadn't I dubbed them Pip, Squeak and Wilfred, the comic characters of my childhood?

When we moved to a house in Kensington that had no garden other than a patio patch on the flat roof of the studio that occupied what had been the garden, all the dogs learned very quickly that they must now go upstairs and through two cat-flaps to empty bowels and bladder (making a daily chore for me), and there was a mad dash to Kensington Gardens at sixish every morning and less regularly at night. Six dogs on leads, three in each hand, were perfectly manageable provided that there was no distraction and no change in ritual, but one summer evening, on entering the gardens to find too many sunbathers just within the gate, I decided that it might be wise to walk a little further than usual before releasing them from their leads; they pulled and yelped, and an elderly woman carrying bags of shopping in both hands walked up to me and with the seraphic countenance of a woman supremely confident that her intended interference will be welcomed, said 'I can help you to control your dogs.' 'I am perfectly in control,' I responded, 'and it is not helpful to stop us when we are so obviously in a hurry to be somewhere less crowded.' The dogs, three leads in each hand and looped – as was my precautionary habit – about my wrists, chose this very moment to change places from left to right and right to left, crossing my arms behind the old dame and compelling me to encircle her in a tight embrace from which, her arms hanging straight to hold her shopping, she could not escape. And there we were, nose to nose at first, then, as the dogs pulled harder, cheek to cheek, she walking very slowly backwards and me forward, praying that we would not topple. Somehow I slipped the leads from my wrists and away ran the dogs, releasing her without accident – and not since Mrs Tiggy-Winkle scuttled naked away up the hill has any old lady vanished in so quick a trice.

At much the same time, Hecate was responsible for a small miracle. An old friend, struck dumb and wholly paralysed by a stroke, was languishing in hospital, unresponsive to any treatment, given no hope of recovery. 'We have made her comfortable,' the Sister said, 'but it's only a matter of time.' On my next visit I smuggled Hecate in under my overcoat, pretending to have a broken arm. Margaret's eyes widened, there was the faint hint of a smile, and for the first time since the blow, she reached out, very very slowly and only an inch or two, to touch the little bitch – and Hecate, usually wriggling wild, quietly settled next to her and lay there motionless. We managed the smuggling a second time, next day, and almost managed it a third, but in came the Sister and there, on the bed, was Hecate. The rage of an uncomprehending senior nurse, armoured by her expert knowledge of disease, health, safety and innumerable regulations, can be magnificent and crushing: Hecate was damned as the vehicle of plague and leprosy, and I as the Devil's henchman. We were forbidden ever to set foot in that Sister's ward again, but it mattered not at all, for we had passed the turning-point in Margaret's recovery – indeed, we had made the turning-point. I am sufficiently convinced of this to argue that in certain circumstances, to take advantage of the mental, emotional and physical benefits, dogs should not only be allowed, but encouraged, to visit patients in hospitals.

Hecate was much given to eating and drinking without thought. No visitor holding a glass of wine with languid arm outstretched could drink his fill, for Hecate, with infinite delicacy, would empty it. With friends for dinner installed in the dining room, Hecate busied herself with the glasses left in the sitting-room and licked them clean, and could later be found asleep in an armchair, belly up, snoring on the dregs of whisky, gin and wine. She was adept at picking ripe raspberries and blackberries, her tongue curled round the fruit, easing it away from the core. She crunched the plastic bottle of my mother's sleeping pills and was discovered deeply unconscious with a purple foam about her lips – I had to slap and shake her while we rushed her to the vet. On one of my returns from Turkey she leaped into the car and refused to be removed; forgetting that there was a bag of unsalted peanuts stashed under my seat for an emergency (common in Turkey), I left her there – she emptied it, a whole kilo swallowed by her tiny frame, there to swell in the moisture of her stomach and, undigested and much larger, be painfully excreted in the small front garden. Then the pigeons flocked, caring not at all for the peanuts' journey through her gut. When the plumber came to mend a pipe, she ate his ball of wire wool, and that, even more painfully, passed through her too; chewing it did her teeth no good and, eventually, most fell out. She went blind, and it was when toothless and blind, but still spritely and beautiful, that in nearby Gloucester Road, an Arab in full Arabian fig asked me how much I wanted for her. I demurred. He produced a sheaf of £50 notes and offered five. I shook my head. He increased the offer. I shook my head again, smiled, held up both hands, fingers spread wide, and backed away.

Running was Hecate's joyful pastime – mostly running for the sake of it, as fast as she could, to and fro along a line, sometimes in increasingly tight circles in which, like a racing motorcyclist, she seemed to be at an angle of forty-five degrees to the ground. She showed little interest in squirrels and pigeons, but one day a complacent wood pigeon ignored her approach until too late and took off too languidly, and she, springing into the air, brought it down and slaughtered it in a flurry of fluttering wings and falling feathers. Moments earlier, children and nannies had been fawning over 'such a dear little doggie', but now they screamed in tears and horror, or buried their faces in the full skirts of furious nannies who threatened me with the majesty of park keepers and policemen.

Hecate's blindness led to a curious and touching relationship with Gamage, the short-legged and barrel-chested pup in Ginny's litter. The same height, but much burlier and heavier, Gamage took to running shoulder-to-shoulder with Hecate, skilfully steering her at speed past trees, people and bicycles. Contact seemed the clue to this; nudging to the left was easy to explain if Gamage was at Hecate's right shoulder – she had only to increase the pressure – but to steer her to the right *from* the right (which is what she often did), required Hecate to bear to the right immediately she could no longer feel the contact. To me this demonstrated extraordinary intelligence on the part of both dogs. I first observed it in 1978 and they practised it until January 1981, the month of Hecate's death.

On 17 January Hecate had a devastating stroke that twisted her little body so that the fore part was at a quarter turn from the rear. She could not walk. In no position could she lie comfortably. And blind, she cannot have understood what had happened to her. She was also doubly incontinent, but for the moment this did not matter to me, though I have no doubt that it mattered to her, for she had always been fastidiously clean and rather private in emptying her bowels and bladder. I needed to know if her twisted body would or might untwist, but Rusty's answer was uncertain. For five nights I slept on the floor next to her, in touch to reassure her, her pathetic little body supported by cushions, lying on absorbent pads that could easily be changed. In eating and drinking she had to be supported and showed little interest in either. For five days there was no improvement, only inexorable deterioration, and Rusty and I decided that he must do the deed, and that deed done, her twisted little body straightened and she seemed as perfect as she had ever been.

I wrapped her in the child's blanket that had long been her comforter, put her in a wicker basket and exposed it on the flat roof of the house where rain, sun and wind reduced her to a perfect skeleton.

≈ 6 ≈

Schubert, Gamage and Spinoza

That Ginevra's daughters were strong and lived long lives
was wholly due to my mother who, having contrived their
siring, made herself entirely responsible for their well-being,
fortifying everything that Ginny ate and drank while pregnant
and, after parturition, throughout their puppyhood, seeking
to enrich her milk; once weaned, the diet of the puppies
too was fortified, to build strong bones. Due on 24 August
1970, Schubert appeared late the night before, Gamage and
Spinoza following in the early hours of the appointed day.
All three lived well into 1986, Schubert departing on 22
June, Gamage exactly a month later, and Spinoza on 20
December (their brother George died on Christmas Eve).
They were healthy animals, their visits to vets very few; their
joints did not creak with arthritis, their teeth did not fall
out, nor did their eyes fail them, and only Gamage, too
enthusiastic an underwater swimmer, was towards the end to
lose her hearing. From them I learned a great deal about the
society of dogs, their interaction and interdependence, their
particular loyalties within their hierarchy (Schubert to Susie,
Gamage to Hecate, Spinoza to Ginny), their shifting sense of
top-doggery when dotage and death come into play, and
their parallel society with humans. Some dogs, I am convinced, are most content when there are enough of them to
have a hierarchy of their own (three are sufficient) in which
the top dog concedes her position, when necessary, to their

owner as *deus ex machina*; others prefer to live as the utterly loyal solitary companion of the cherished human donor of affection and food; between these two extremes are all sorts of variations, combinations and confusions.

With their grandmother, Susie, behaving with all the scheming malevolence of a Byzantine Empress in the Dark Ages, infanticide her clear intention, Ginny and her pups were sequestered in a big spare bedroom, the door locked, for Susie knew very well how to operate a door handle. Time passed, the puppies grew and it was Susie's turn to be locked in while they were let loose in the adventure of the garden for the rest of that long fine summer shading into autumn, and at two months or so I began, tentatively, to introduce the little bitches to the old dowager. With the two dog puppies gone, her murderous mood seemed almost to have evaporated and, apart from occasional harrumphs of annoyance when Gamage (the most persistently playful of her grandchildren) attempted to chew her tail, and snarls at some even worse impertinence, little recalled the menace of her earlier behaviour; nor did she resort to the obstinate sulking and hiding with which she had worn me down when Hecate first came to the house. The watchful sequestering was at an end, all doors were open, the puppies had the freedom of the house and the old dogs taught them the niceties of emptying their bowels and bladders in the garden.

Their passage from puppies into adolescents and from adolescents into adults was uneventful. At six months they were spayed, primarily to frustrate any attempt my mother might make to perpetuate the Susie-Ginny-Spinoza line into a fourth generation, but also to prevent the difficulties inevitable with other dogs in Kensington Gardens – and with their owners – if I failed to notice the early signs of their coming into season, either concurrently or, much worse, in sequence, for the sexually attractive odours of one bitch are carried by others in close contact with her. Having long ago and in ignorance of the canine facts of life failed to impose purdah on Penny, I knew of the scorn, derision and contempt that are heaped on the owner whose bitch is coming into heat without his realising it. Everyone who has walked a bitch in season in a public place knows that the consequence is a following of male dogs, expectant and excited, to the embarrassment of all their owners. Kensington Gardens is, in the early morning when most dogs and their owners are about, a decorous place frequented by decorous people united in the single purpose of exercising their dogs – even the princely and ducal occupants of Kensington Palace walk their own dogs, watched by their inconspicuous guardians – but a single bitch on heat can disrupt both purpose and decorum, for the pheromonal perfumes, wafted on the breeze, alert not just the odd male dog encountered, but every dog from Notting Hill to Knightsbridge and Marloes Road to Marble Arch, and they come running, distraught owners panting after them. Such a disorderly gathering is not easily dispersed, for no lusty hound will walk away unless securely leashed and they all play catch as catch can with their furious owners; nor is it dispersed by picking up one's bitch and slinging her over a shoulder – the man who does that risks having half-a-dozen priapic curs conjugating with his trousers; and if the bitch and her owner are first to escape, they leave behind them a horde of frustrated males inclined to turn to sodomy – an even worse embarrassment.

As their characters developed it was clear that Schubert,

the beauty of the bunch, larger than her mother but almost as whippety and much the same colour, was also the dumb blonde, the last to chase a ball, retrieve a stick or recognise that a strange activity might be a game; she could easily outrun her sisters, but she rarely did, for she was always last to realise that running was expected; she leaped to great heights, but seemed never to take the coming-down into consideration, and I blamed her in some part for Gamage's deafness, for she was always last into the water, almost always ducking Gamage by jumping onto her back. Gamage, on the other hand, the Plain Jane of the trio, stocky and stout, her face and muzzle broad, a black mongrel revealing nothing of the whippet in her ancestry, was extraordinarily intelligent and, like Hecate, was able to relate the interior and exterior of the house – both dogs climbed perilously onto the lean-to roof of the kitchen to bark for attention at a bedroom window if they thought they had been forgotten. Short-legged, she could not spring into my arms, as could her sisters, but if – when she wished – I stood bent double facing away from her, she then leaped onto my back and, as I slowly stood erect, scrabbled her way onto my shoulder and then into my arms; and I loved having her there, for she was warm and soft and cuddly, with none of Schubert's knees and elbows.

Schubert and Gamage appointed themselves part of my family and joined Susie and Hecate on my bed. Spinoza had had just as much of my whispered endearments and cuddling, but she elected to join her mother on my mother's bed, drink tea and become a lap-dog. On walks she joined her sisters, but I discerned a certain disdain for their boisterous wrestling with fallen branches too big to carry, and would never plunge into the Serpentine – though once the others were in after a

stick or swimming simply for the joy of it, she might just
consent to get her forepaws wet. Entirely brindle, she was an
elegant creature, but there was a wildness of eye for which I
did not much care and she was far too ready to growl at the
genital enquiries of other dogs. Very fleet of foot, she was
usually first in any race with her sisters, but that was in part
due to Schubert's dimwittedness. There was a regular course
for their racing on the east side of the Serpentine just short of
the Italian fountains of the Long Water, an acre or so of long
rough grass and seedlings set aside for ground-nesting birds,
enclosed by iron railings and wire netting to exclude the feral
cats that lodged nearby, terrorising the local wildfowl (foxes
had not then invaded inner London). I and the older dogs
kept to the path that separated the enclosure from the Long
Water, but the three sisters set off, as though in response to a
starting-gun, to race round it, out of sight until they rounded
the corner back onto the path in a mad final sprint to greet us
as though they were Stanleys and we Livingstones; and then
Gamage would slink off to begin the round again without
her sisters' immediately realising it and with a reasonable
chance that, in spite of her shorter legs, she might be first to
complete the second circuit. Spinoza and Schubert tucked
their ears neatly back and ran like greyhounds, but Gamage,
to have any chance of keeping up with them, had developed
a stride that appeared to involve her spine as much as her
short legs and, her ears trailing and flapping in the wind,
rather than run she seemed to bounce along the ground in a
series of elongated leaps.

Life in Kensington Gardens in the 1970s and 1980s was
much as it had been when I was a child before World War
II: serene, habitual, subtly changing only with the seasons;
wild geese flew in, rested and flew on, eccentric ducks chose

to nest in trees, leaves budded and leaves fell to be gathered into great mounds and burned, and frost and snow trans-formed the view from Paul Maitland's ethereal autumns into Pissarro's bolder winters. The geese, grazing on grass, deposited pungent juicy stools on which dogs love to roll, returning to their owners patched with what Aldous Huxley described as 'the goose-turd green' of the Trecento Italian Madonna, clods of the revolting stuff jammed under their collars. None of my dogs ever interfered with the ducks' business of coaxing their duckling broods, sometimes hundreds of yards from the shrubberies to the south, to the Round Pond, and once all watched fascinated by a duck on the ground as ducklings scooted backwards and forwards on the reaching branch of a great tree in answer to her call, plucking up courage to drop the thirty feet or so to join her, the tiny balls of down then righting themselves and running to the shelter of her wings. Bitches, I am inclined to say, have such powerful mothering instincts that they tend to protect the infants of any species – and twice on early morning walks mine found litters of kittens among the bushes and, mightily agitated, seemed to insist that they be carried home (and they were).

There were occasional disruptions to serenity – too many nursemaids, the sunbathers and courting couples whom the dogs regarded as obstacles over whom to leap at speed, interrupting coitus, a profusion of bicycles and, once a year, the annual gathering of grown men, grey and grizzled, who met to race their model yachts – not toys, but models as much as six feet long, fully rigged, every timber varnished, their brass accoutrements gleaming. In Lilliputian perfection these set sail on diametrical courses across the pond while their solitary captains walked briskly round to greet them on the further shore. Were they all old admirals dreaming of times past? On such a day the Round Pond was no place for dogs but, tempted by the shouts of these mariners to look at the event, since I too, in my childhood, had similarly set sail in my imagination (particularly to Java and Sumatra) though with smaller craft crudely made with a fretsaw, I drew too close, and Schubert and Gamage, accustomed to leaping into the Serpentine, rushing as fast as they could, sprang into the pond careless of the consequences. In terms of naval battles, victory was theirs, the casualties three ships turned turtle, their sails lying sodden in the water and Lord knows what damage done to their rigging.

When, in 1978, Henry Moore exhibited two dozen major sculptures on the lawns of Kensington Gardens (an ugly visual assault of insufferable arrogance), accompanying every one of them was a notice forbidding the touch of human hand, but curators had forgotten the interest that dogs would inevitably show in them, taking them to be objects on which they must deposit urine. My bitches were not alone in this; every passing dog lifted his leg to add to the palimpsest of urinary calling cards, and every bitch hitched her buttocks as high as she could to leave her dribbling trace. I have wondered ever since if, when returned to the pastures of Much Hadham, Henry noticed an interesting change in patination here and there: convinced that the first emptying of the bladder in the morning, richer in nutrients than all later emptyings, produced the very best of natural patinas, Matisse (another occasional maker of bronzes) kept his fresh casts in his garden, sometimes for years, so that he could pee on them.

All my dogs were occasionally taken out for the day, to Hampstead Heath, Wimbledon Common, Richmond Park and Box Hill, as well as for weekends in Winchelsea. The day trips involved picnicking – setting up camp, as it were – a point at which the dogs always became territorial if other dogs came near, sustained low growling and the sudden dashing feint the consequence, the grabbing of collars some-times necessary. I am convinced that their daily walks are much more than physical exercise – that they are intellectual stimulus too, the equivalent of our reading the morning newspaper; it is a great mistake to urge on a dog when it pauses for a snuffle, to keep a brisk and unforgiving pace or, worse still, to run or ride a bicycle with the dog constantly playing catch-up, for a dog does not merely walk, it sees and sniffs, analyses and records – and if that is the equivalent of *The Times*, then an adventurous walk over unfamiliar territory is the equivalent of a novel by P. D. James or Francis King that intrigues, thrills, excites, amuses and is a business as much of the mind as of the body. Creatures of habit they may be, perhaps by preference, but take them to pastures new and in their body language their cerebral response is at once evident.

With a skiing, walking, clambering and tennis-playing friend I took Schubert and Gamage to Dartmoor in the late summer of 1979. We stayed at the Lydford Arms on the west side of the Moor where villages and roads are fewest, intending to climb the high tors. On the first afternoon, to recover from the long drive and encourage an appetite for dinner, we followed the river up Lydford Gorge where what had been a shallow stream narrowed and tumbled between rocks – and it was at this point that Gamage, fifty yards ahead, jumped in. For a moment she disappeared, somersaulted by the turbulence, but then, head up, using her forepaws to deflect her from crashing into boulders, riding the current, she swept past us; I ran back to overtake

her, ready to jump in and retrieve the body of my drowned
dog, but long before I could, the stream widened, curved
and slowed, forming a few feet of sandy bank, and there she
grounded, emerged, shook herself and came running back to
me for a rapturous embrace. We resumed our walk up the
gorge, the dogs much closer, but when we were almost back
at the point where this shooting-the-rapids escapade had
begun, Gamage ran ahead and began the game again, this
time completely in command, her foresight and judgement
perfect as she fended herself from every rock – and when she
reached the shallows, out she climbed again.

Every day we walked some twenty or twenty-five miles,
one of our loops across the Moor so underestimated in terms
of obstacles – bracken shoulder high and, in the rain, passable
only by leaning backwards into it, flattening it enough to
take a pace – that, exhausted, we were compelled to find a
taxi willing to take us, sodden to the skin, and two equally
sodden and muddy dogs, back to Lydford. Gamage was far
more sensible than Schubert; she immediately fathomed the
complexities of clambering over a stile, realised that to the
side of every sheep barrier in a track there is always a way
through a hedge or over a wall, and it was she who sensed
that what was on the far side of a wall that could, from the
near side, easily be jumped, must not be assumed to be on
the same level or even of the same firm earth – she always
jumped onto a wall rather than over it. Gamage also always
lay full length and rested whenever we paused to consult
a map or light a cigarette, but Schubert surged about,
expending energy. Poor Schubert – her approach to obstacles
was one of petrifear, that is standing stock still but trembling
with anxiety and indecision, followed by an unconsidered
dash at stile, sheep-trap or wall, calamity quite certain.

We climbed the tors, revisited Grey Wethers – but the dogs did not respond, as Susie had, with signs of fear – viewed the looming bulk of Princetown Prison from a distance, found a lost hunting hound and returned it to its kennels (an alarming experience for Schubert and Gamage – so many surging hounds, so big, so threatening, so noisy), came across a dead pony rotting in a stream – but then Dartmoor is a place of death in that one can hardly walk a mile without finding a bleached skull or the shreds of some small furred or feathered body. Later, we moved south, away from the unfriendly Moor – beautiful in its way but never welcoming, and if the fine weather changed to wind and rain, quite hazardous – stayed in Hope Cove and walked the coastal paths where poor Schubert had to come to terms with jetties and ferries and being dropped into small boats or passed from my trusted arms into those of strange sailors one after another. There were occasions when the waves were bucking beneath the wide gaps of missing planks in jetties when I'd swear she committed her soul to a Higher Power and abandoned the will to live.

It was the last long walk, for within a year the three sisters were into double figures and a twenty-mile trek is too much for a dog of ten and more; nor were there weekends at Winchelsea, for the house there had been sold, compelling me to exhume the bones of Ginny and Susie – a sad handful in each case, frail armatures difficult to relate to the warmth and beauty of their bodies; with these I again climbed to the roof of the house and gently put them in the wicker basket that was Hecate's tomb; of her, nothing but shreds of skin and a complete skeleton were left. Their whiskers whitened, they slowed down, lost interest in the waters of the Serpentine, and a morning or an afternoon, sans picnic, was enough if we drove to Wimbledon or Richmond. When mice invaded the house, only Gamage dealt with them, presenting me with a tiny body whenever she caught one; the invasion lasted less than a month; neither Schubert nor Spinoza showed interest or instinct.

In June 1986 Schubert lost interest in food and water, fell asleep and did not wake again; for three days she lay on the dogs' couch in the kitchen, an ancient and comfortable wicker thing with deep cushions in which they nestled, and emitted occasional groans that wrenched my heart; Rusty gave me pills with which to deepen her sleep and on the third evening, with me sitting beside her, reading, my right hand on her shoulder, she died. I did not feel her go; there was no final tremor, no sense of a last breath – nothing – but I thought I sensed a drop in temperature and the faint heaving of her chest had stopped; there was no sign of breath on the chill mirror.

Six months before, the friend who had owned the house in Winchelsea sent me an enormous hamper, and when Schubert died I hauled the basket onto the roof for her interment; in it, wrapped in a blanket, though the largest of the sisters, she seemed very small, but I sensed that, just short of sixteen, she would not long be alone. Within a month Gamage seemed indefinably unwell and I took her to Rusty; I wish that I had not. He diagnosed some internal problem, operated, found it to be incurable and telephoned to tell me; I said what I was compelled to say and drove at once to collect her body, warm and limp, and cursed myself for letting her suffer Susie's death among strangers in the clinical circumstances of the surgery rather than in my arms and at home. What is the point of a vow if one does not keep it? I let the surgery door close behind me, sat on his doorstep and howled with grief.

Spinoza, now my only dog, very frail and very grizzled, continued the daily discipline of a walk in Kensington Gardens, but I had sometimes to carry her there and carry her home, and we went very early on dark winter mornings to escape encounters with more boisterous dogs. Six months after Schubert's death she too refused food and water, fell into a coma and, like her sister but more swiftly, died beside me. I was writing in my study, sitting on a couch in the bay window, pen and paper on my lap (as is my custom), and I had lifted her onto the neighbouring cushion; the very faint sound of a movement of her tail alerted me – not quite a wag but more than a twitch – and she too was gone.

With Spinoza's going my misery was absolute. It was not just for her that I mourned – indeed she was the sister I liked least – but for silly Schubert, the beauty of the litter, stout Gamage, the most staunch of friends, for Ginevra their mother and Susannah their grandmother, for Hecate who had witnessed their birth, and for Trollop, a deserted bitch whom they had discovered tied to the railings of the Flower Walk in Kensington Gardens.

7

Trollop

Trollop, from 15 May 1976 until 17 February 1985, was the outsider of the pack, but her tale begins with that of another bitch, five years earlier. I had just done some heavy shopping in Kensington's first supermarket and as I emerged onto the High Street saw a young dog running eastward between the two streams of traffic, trailing what I took to be a lead from her collar. To an elderly woman standing nearby I said, peremptorily, 'Look after these for me,' dumped my shopping at her feet, ran through the traffic and grabbed the dog. She had neither collar nor lead; what I had taken to be these were a length of rope bound so tight about her neck and face that it had pressed a furrow in her muzzle and she could not open her mouth to breathe or pant – the only means a dog has of controlling its temperature. For the moment, however, the rope was a convenience and, having collected my bags from their bemused guardian, I took the dog home.

Perhaps nine months old, filthy and starving, this little bitch I bathed and combed, cleared her coat of live fleas and as many of their eggs as I could find, and fed her some chicken by hand. Later she had other small meals and I kept her overnight. I should have kept her longer – indeed I should simply have kept her, but the law then dictated that a stray dog, perhaps an animal for which its owner had bought a licence, should be taken to the police – and so, fed yet again, the following day I took her to Earl's Court Police Station. 'Do you wish to keep her if she is not claimed?' asked the officer. Taken by surprise, I refused, and he then said that she would be kept and cared for in the station until the end of the following day and then sent to the pound.

In the late morning of the following day I returned to the station. I had by then learned that at the pound she had only seven days in which to be found by her old owner or adopted by a new, and would then be put down. I thought of the roped muzzle and the suffering it must have caused her, of her filthy and starved condition, and concluded that I had been a thoughtless fool in respecting the law, and that I had been responsible for condemning her to two terrible alternatives – either a life of cruel mistreatment at the hands of her legitimate owner, or almost immediate death. I could bear neither thought. The officer told me that the pound van had been early that day and had already collected her. To my 'Where is the pound?' there was no clear answer – 'It depends which one had room for her . . . no, there is no list . . . no, we have no telephone numbers . . . you are not the owner and have no right to such information . . . ' I spent the rest of the day in hopeless pursuit and, in misery, gave up.

That little bitch was my first thought when the three sisters discovered Trollop tied to the inner railings of the Flower Walk. They were always finding creatures in need of human assistance – dumped kittens, snared rabbits, baby crows and starlings, a moorhen with its feet bitten off, and countless damaged ducks and pigeons. All these could be mended or despatched and none became permanent members of the household, but dogs are different – they tend to stick. Someone had taken this one to Kensington Gardens the previous evening shortly before the gates were closed, calculated that he would not be seen if he tied her to the inner railings to which no path ran close and shrubbery offered camouflage, and walked away. It had been a cold wet night – indeed a drenching night – there was no shelter and her thick coat was sodden to the skin. Untied, she lay where she was, indifferent to the interest of the three sisters (Hecate was not with us – the weather was too foul for her), unwilling to stand or walk; I picked her up – a bag of bones – threw her over my shoulder and went home. My mother, sometimes given to Satanic mysteries, at once decided that she was a reincarnation of the little lost bitch, though there was not the slightest resemblance, for she had been a mongrel not unlike Gamage, and Trollop (called so because I found that she was on heat) was clearly of Alsatian stock. This time there was no question of what should be done – she had to stay. I thought her about a year old, experiencing her second heat and probably thrown out because of it (with some bitches it is a messy and volatile business). She seemed terrified of entering the house and must, I think, have been kept in an open yard. For weeks she could not find the coordination to climb stairs, and it was months before she dared clamber onto furniture; when she wanted to sleep, she just flopped on the floor, making no distinction between cold tiles in the kitchen and the carpets in my study. Television and my typewriter fascinated her and she often reached forward, always with her right paw, and jammed the keys – are dogs left- and right-handed?

My mother's diary for 15 May 1976 records her as 'poor darling; she was in such a sorry state, dishevelled and starving' – but not for long. Her coat grew very thick and glossy, and when, later in the year, we found a kitten in Kensington Gardens, it was Trollop who took to caring for him, carrying him by the scruff of his neck between her teeth, and letting him sleep curled in the dense fur of her chest and under her chin. Though bigger than the sisters, and far bigger than Hecate, she was obviously bottom dog throughout her life, occasionally bullied, particularly by Spinoza, and yet made no attempt to better her status in the pack, content to be an outsider – as, to some extent, was Hecate who, throughout their common lives, snuggled with her like the kitten, a pretty contrast worthy of Landseer as the subject of a painting.

Never once did Trollop snarl or growl at her companions and she was amiable with every dog we met – even when attacked by a vicious Jack Russell she did not retaliate. It was early on a Saturday morning when most dog-walkers spend an extra hour in bed and there are few about; neither dog nor owner had we encountered before – nor did we again – and the attack was a surprise. In a single continuous move-ment the terrier ran fast at Trollop from fifty yards away, bit her right flank just below the rib cage, and ran off to circle her and repeat the movement, but in this second run I sought to fend him off and he bit me. There I stood, the terrier hanging from my right hand, his teeth sunk deep into the fat cushion of flesh below the thumb, shouting at the dog's owner, a post-military type in tweeds, with cap and walking stick, still fifty yards away, standing stock still – and then there was a blank. The pain extreme, I felt the dread nausea of a faint creep up on me, sank to the ground and put my head between my knees. When I recovered, both the Jack Russell and the military man had disappeared. From too cursory an inspection of Trollop's flank I concluded that her thick coat had protected her and, hugely relieved that the malevolent terrier had attacked her rather than one of the thin-skinned others (he could have killed Hecate) and that mine was the only wound, I wrapped my hand tightly in a handkerchief, tucked it into my shirt, and we walked on.

At home it was to my hand that I first paid attention, recalling some old wives' tale about the fatality inevitable when a man is wounded where the terrier had bitten me, but then I noticed that Trollop was licking her flank. I found a clean cut in her skin below the fur, some two inches long and clearly in need of stitches. As to drive to the vet involved a cat's cradle of one-way streets and the risk of a jam in the High Street, we walked, ten minutes on foot. The injury was more serious than I had thought and there was sub-cutaneous damage to repair before the cut could be stitched, but Rusty was alone, without a nurse, and Trollop must have an anaesthetic. 'You will have to play nurse,' he said, 'can you do that?'

I could, did, and with the mending done, found myself in the street with a still unconscious Trollop in my arms, trying to hail a cab. A man dressed in the precautionary clothes of the dog-walker (that is, ready for any mishap involving mud and blood) rather than the peacockery of the *passeggio* that is the shopping mode for such places as Kensington and Wimbledon on Saturdays, and particularly one who appears to be carrying a dead dog, is not an attractive client for a cabby. As none stopped, I began to walk home. A conscious dog, no matter how weak, contributes to her being carried and in clinging with her forelegs and distributing her weight, seems lighter than she is; an unconscious dog, however, is to all intents and purposes a dead dog and weighs exactly what she weighs. Trollop, moreover, had to be carried so that her wound was neither stretched nor cramped – that is, flat; thus she was supported on my forearms, locked in a right angle –

as it were – at the elbow, her head and hindquarters hanging beyond them, to the passer-by looking very dead, their time-consuming expressions of sympathy a damned nuisance on this trek. Cramps and aches began and I longed to sit and rest my forearms on my knees, but there were no low garden walls, no friendly benches, and when, at last, I came upon a car with a bonnet low enough on which to hitch my buttocks for a minute, it was a Ferrari with an uncharitably shrill burglar alarm.

Trollop was the sweetest, gentlest and least wilful of dogs. On finding a pigeon with a broken wing she brought it to me without further damage and I took it home to mend and heal, keeping it in my bath, and there she inspected it several times a day. And when a disoriented duck led eight ducklings into the garden of a particularly scatterbrained neighbour opposite, it was Trollop who discovered their hiding-places and helped me trap them in a box – imagine her bringing the tiny creatures to me in her mouth; that done, a keeper from Kensington Gardens came to catch the duck and, reunited with her family, all were taken off to live on the pool in the Sunken Garden of Kensington Palace. Trollop should have been an only dog, for though she played, romped and ran as much as Schubert, Spinoza and Gamage when we were out and about, she seemed utterly lacking in any competitive element and always relinquished the ball, stick or whatever else might be the toy of the moment and returned to me as though they and their games were of no serious interest; she was always the dog on my bed, but they occasionally slept elsewhere. 'Dear, darling, lovable Trollop . . .' wrote my mother in her diary on the day of Trollop's death – a death that came too soon.

In the late autumn of 1984, when I had had her for eight

years, she began to flounder – I can think of no other word for her momentary clumsiness, her unaccountable overruns and misjudgements of the stairs. Hardly noticeable at first, they rapidly grew worse and, though five years younger than the now elderly sisters, she withdrew from their activities and plodded at my heels. There was no obvious reason for her disability, but Rusty found it interesting and he saw her regularly as the stumbling worsened, though without ever suggesting that he knew what was wrong. I was more than alarmed when she began to drag her paws in such a way that, eventually, her knuckles bled and I could no longer bear to walk her on pavements – indeed, she so evidently got no pleasure from walking that, at hours when almost no one was about (and breaking all the rules), I let her into the garden of the church at the end of the road so that she could totter about on the grass. By early February 1985 she had lost the use of all four legs and could hardly stand. In the late afternoon of the seventeenth, a Sunday, seeming very bewildered, she ate a few slivers of chicken and I then lifted her onto my bed and sat with her head in my lap, wondering what to do, miserable. I called Rusty, discussed the certainties, and he, saintly man, said that he would come within an hour – but within that hour, imperceptibly, she died, so quietly, so quietly.

He asked for her body. He had done many tests and sent many samples to a laboratory in Cambridge, and had every right to ask, now that she was dead, to send her body there so that scientists might inspect her brain – for the first time he suggested that it might be a cerebral problem. I should have given my consent, but the thought of her beautiful head sawn asunder on a pathologist's cold slab appalled me and I refused. This was an irrational response, but I had loved her so intensely that the integrity of her body was to me, for the immediate moment, more important than cold science. I was a sentimental fool. I did not think of possible benefit to other animals. Years later, when Mad Cow Disease swept the agricultural industry, I thought that I recognised in the hapless stumbling of cattle exactly Trollop's symptoms.

It was Trollop who led to my discovering Catkin in July 1978. On entering or leaving the house she took to standing on the front steps looking over the wall into the garden next door, and one day, in the spirit of enquiry, I stood with her and was rewarded by the fleeting glimpse of a small tabby cat peeping from the disused coal-hole under my neighbour's steps. More watching led to my seeing that the cat was feral and pregnant, and this led to my leaving food, milk and water for her on my own front steps, to the incomprehension of the dogs. These I did not, for many days, see her consume, and wondered if some other cat had been the beneficiary, and then, at last, saw her returning to her lair carrying in her jaws the small plastic dish of dog food. There were six kittens – or rather, I once saw six tiny kittens basking in the sun – but one by one the number was reduced: were they taken for food by other feral cats, did the little queen eat them herself (surely unlikely as I was feeding her), or were they dying of some disease (a feline form of tuberculosis, perhaps) in that damp coal-hole? When only one was left, a tiny tabby queen the image of her mother, on 7 September, I caught her and gave her to a sympathetic neighbour (with whom she lived for eighteen years).

Catkin, as I lamely dubbed her, promptly disappeared, but a year later she was back, again pregnant. Had she remembered my help with her previous pregnancy? I resumed the rigmarole of feeding her, five strong kittens the consequence, first seen, again in a patch of sunlight, on 12 September 1979. A month later, after accustoming her to collecting her food from within the front door (was I ever as patient with any human?), I trapped her between it and the inner door, caught the five kittens, gave one to another interested neighbour, drove the remaining four to a cat-rescue home, and took the furious Catkin to the vet to be spayed. She is the only animal of whom I have been truly scared: in the box-room space between the doors she growled and spat and clawed, her belligerent moves quite unpredictable; I had never heard a cat growl and from so small an animal it seemed an awful sound, and I wished that I had worn my reading glasses, for I feared for my sight – indeed I feared for my throat too, for the little cat had turned into a tiger. Somehow I got her into the box given me by the vet, but I felt less triumphant when I brought her back, for she made straight for the coal-hole and began a piteous yowling.

I thought she would disappear again, but she did not. From a friendly painter who was more carpenter than artist I commissioned a home for her, and he made a Roman basilica with a pedimented entrance, the roof hinged so that I could refresh the sheepskin that was to be her bedding. It stood on my doorstep sheltered by a canopy, and from its entrance she could see the world pass by. Within a week she had taken residence and ignored the comings and goings of five dogs. Within a month the Blunt Affair erupted and with fifty journalists laying siege to my door I feared that she might flee, but she now had confidence and stayed where she was. The change was remarkable and to me a thing of great pleasure; never did she come into the house, but if I sat on the doorstep very still, she deigned from time to time to sit beside me and permit a gentle stroke – but these encounters always ended with a sudden hiss or a cuff of the paw, as though to remind me (and herself) that she was no man's cat, but a free spirit.

Even so, she attached herself to the nightly walk round the block with the dogs, several paces behind them, ready to duck into a garden if we met other dogs on the same errand. That the dogs tolerated this, even, once the business was established, expected it and were dismayed if Catkin was absent on some more feline mission, proved to me that dogs are intelligent enough to do almost anything to please their masters, even if it is counter-intuitive. As for the intelligence of cats – when one of my snootier neighbours at the back of the house (one of Mrs Thatcher's lordlings) ostentatiously hung a brace of pheasant outside his kitchen, Catkin stole them and brought them to my door, quite edible, though their feathers were tattered by her having to clamber over walls and drag them along pavements. And it was pretty bright of Catkin to take a lodger, a brawny Tom with so much scar tissue in his cheeks that his face was unnaturally wide and quite out of proportion with his shoulders, who noisily defended her from other toms. He was called Tom because he was the archetypal roving, fighting, cock-o'-the-walk tom cat and neither Tancred not Torquil would have suited him.

In the hot summer of 1984, on 7 July, I found Catkin dead on my front steps; she had clearly been hit by a car, had made her way home and died in a last effort to climb them, her body reaching over three steps. I followed drops of blood on the pavement to the point where she had crossed the road from the church garden where she often basked; it is a cul-de-sac where no resident would drive dangerously fast. I climbed to the roof with her, to lie in Hecate's basket, where she too became an immaculate skeleton.

To my surprise, when I opened the door to feed Tom he came into the house and abandoned the basilica – it remained on the step but no other cat came to occupy it. Tom remained my house cat until shortly before the death of Titian, my next dog, to whom he was devoted, ten years later. A strange phenomenon, the close friendship between so very male a cat and so very male a dog, but not quite close enough – Tom still had tom-cat things to do and occasionally was away for a day or so on some amatory errand, and from one of them he did not return.

⤞ 8 ⤝

Titian and Mrs Macbeth

With the death of Spinoza in December 1986, I was cast down with greater grief than ever before. For more than a quarter of a century Susie and her descendants had rampaged through all other aspects of my life and now none of them was left to impose her disciplines on mine. I was oddly unprepared for such emptiness and silence in the house; three deaths in a year, all to be expected with dogs from the same litter, sixteen years a goodly span, should have steeled my emotions, but they had not, even though, for the last months of Spinoza's life I had so evidently been living in the growing shadow of her death. Over the most miserable Christmas I had rejected the urgings of friends that I must at once 'get another dog', as though losing Spinoza was no worse than a clumsy fall while skiing and – as the skier must – I should put myself together again and schuss down the nearest black piste. Halfway through January, however, Rusty Williams telephoned. A dog had been brought to the surgery to be put down though in good health, aged six or so, about Schubert's size, but a little heavier; his elderly mistress had died and neighbours had brought him in. 'A dog?' I warily enquired. 'Not a bitch? I've never had a dog. I'm not sure that I want one.' To this, Rusty's reply was, more or less, that my refusal to take him on would be the end of him.

That evening, 14 January 1987, indecently soon after Spinoza's death, Rusty delivered him. His coat light tan and much the same as Schubert's, short, silken and whippety, his ribs visible in terms, not of undernourishment, but fitness, his tail not docked, he was heavy for the whippet who may have been one parent and light for the boxer who may have been the other, for he had something of a boxer's muzzle, broader than Schubert's and with the undershot jaw of the Hapsburgs. The old lady whose companion he had been had called him Keegan, after a celebrated footballer – and that was the first thing that I had to eliminate from his past. The Hapsburg jaw prompted the thought of Charles V, the Holy Roman Emperor so sensitively painted by Titian, and 'Titian' seemed a sound not so far from Keegan that the change would be difficult for a middle-aged dog to accommodate; at every opportunity I sat with him beside me or half-draped across my lap and spoke the word into his ear – 'Your name is Titian.' It is not that he knew the words, but I am convinced that he knew their sense. The other problem was the freedom to which he had been accustomed – his old mistress, too frail to exercise him, had simply opened a window onto the street and let him wander on his own. It was thus immediately impossible to leave a window open; this hardly mattered in the arctic blizzard conditions of January 1987, but later in the year, the house, facing south onto the street, would become intolerably hot, and I soon observed that Titian, who investigated every window in the house and would, I am sure, have risked leaping from the attic, was a most determined dog.

Within days I learned in Kensington Gardens that his response to a bitch in the merest hint of heat was of single-minded randiness that meant for me a sprinting pursuit towards the far horizon, that all male puppies and adolescent dogs must be sodomised, and that towards all mature dogs his aggression was barely suppressed. I have seen unaccompanied dogs use pedestrian crossings with humans to whom they do not belong, but I think myself the only driver who would pay a dog alone the required courtesy of stopping. Most dogs cross roads at whim, and cross the main Kensington road Titian did, twice within the first two weeks, having escaped me on some compelling purpose of his own, and also having street wisdom enough to find his way to his new home – but no one who has seen a dog rolled under a car and left with four broken legs can reasonably argue in favour of street freedom for man's best friend.

Within three weeks I had had almost enough of Titian. I had failed to cure his other vice – of raiding waste bins from which anything edible, no matter how foul, must be swallowed at a gulp and regurgitated on a carpet, my bed or a settee – and a catastrophic walk in Kensington Gardens was the breaking point. On this, though my only dog and the sole object of my concentration, he had again contrived to disappear and test the limits of my patience and the time to be spent shouting 'Titian' to a dog almost certainly out of earshot. An hour later than usual I returned home, angry and despairing, again to find him waiting at my gate. I could have beaten him, so angry was I, but instead picked him up, carried him into the house and sat with him on the stairs, hugging him very close – and then I talked to him in plain English. I told him that I had had my fill of his ingratitude and waywardness, that he had exceeded the bounds of tolerance, and that if he continued with such misbehaviour he would have to go – back to the vet, to a police pound, to an almost certain death – but that he could not stay with me; then, suddenly I felt the tension leave his body – still in my tight hug, he relaxed, and when I too relaxed, he settled and laid his head in my lap. I cannot claim that thereafter he was perfectly behaved – indeed, to reduce his aggression towards other adult males I had eventually to consent to the chemical 'castration' suggested by Rusty – but he became at once a more manageable dog.

'Manageable' did not mean that he became obedient – only that he seemed to recognise that he and I had a particular relationship, probably of equals, but that there were moments, recognisable in the timbre of my voice, when immediate compliance was politic, and if a shade too late, then he must perform the canine rituals of apology. After he stole a great wedge of prime Cheddar cheese riven by the blue vein that (in my view) sharpens the strong flavour, the mouldy rind reinforced by fine threads of cheese-cloth wrapping, two whole pounds of it from Paxton & Whitfield, I learned never to leave food within his reach – he ate it, every crumb, his tummy swollen tight, groaning with the ache of it (punishment enough), but I knew full well that, given the opportunity, he would eat it all again. If friends came to stay and, greeting me with a friendly hug, dropped their luggage where we stood, Titian laid claim by emptying his bladder on it (difficult to explain on a dry day); I learned to spurn their hugs, seize their bags and hurry them away. Titian formed a passionate sexual relationship with the settee in my study, a good and comfortable old thing covered in yellow velvet that would have lasted another half century had it not been for his attentions; velvet will tolerate just so much sponging and mopping of ejaculate, and cushions reach a point when they cannot again be turned; eventually the settee had to go and was carried away by a charity that donated used furniture to the indigent. Deprived of it, Titian discovered the pleasures of auto-fellatio, performing it as a party trick, it seemed, whenever women were in the house.

During one of those 'weeks' when all Londoners are supposed to collaborate in corporate activity – a pyjama week, a red-nose week, a take-your-baby-to-work week and, on this occasion, a take-your-pet-to-work week – I took Titian to the offices of the *Evening Standard*. 'You can't bring him in here,' said the commissionaire. 'But it's bring-your-dog-to-work week,' I protested. 'Not here it ain't,' his gruff reply. I pleaded. He relented if I promised not to take more than ten minutes. I could tie Titian to the stout leg of a console table that was an integral part of the extravagant marble decoration of the entrance hall, and dash up the escalator to the second floor. His lead shortened by the tying, I thought Titian would retreat under the table, but he did not; he strained against the leg and his howls turned to urgent barks as I disappeared up the escalator, echoing throughout the atrium, even to the sanctums of the powerful on the sixth floor, where no ordinary mortal trod and few dare speak above a whisper.

I had only to deliver the typescript of an article, an errand of two minutes, but time enough for chaos to develop. As I left my desk Titian was still barking, but now with a frantic timbre, and as I ran down the escalator I could see why, for in the hall below was a canine version of Samson's destruction of the house of the Philistines. Titian was still tethered to the leg of the table, but only to the leg, and was now backed into a corner preparing to do battle with the commissionaire and his deputy. In his desperation to follow me he had pulled so hard that the columnar leg had come away from its sockets and the heavy marble slab lay shattered on the marble floor. I untied him and we fled.

He had two friends, one close, the other distant. Tom –

the stray cat – was close. They often slept together and daily played a game that, had they been children, would have been 'Wheelbarrows'; in this, Titian stalked Tom until, perfectly positioned, he could ram his head between the cat's hind legs, lifting his hindquarters so that his weight rested wholly on his forepaws, and then steered him hither and yon until they reached the top of the stairs to the kitchen; there Titian tossed his head and the hapless Tom was sent tumbling, bumpety-bump, not recovering until he reached the floor below. The distant friend was Mrs Macbeth, no lady, but an elderly Jack Russell bitch of constantly murderous intent. Rusty Williams, knowing nothing of my early difficulties with Titian, telephoned to ask if I would like to rescue another dog brought into his surgery to be put down, perceived as perhaps a menace to a new baby, ten years old, in fine shape, but small for the Jack Russell that she was. I could not refuse, and I thought that a bitch in the house might soothe the restless Titian. She arrived in the evening of 3 February 1987, brought by her distressed mistress, her name Penny. The farewells done, I went down to the kitchen to prepare supper and Penny promptly sank her teeth into my right hand; when she let go, streaming blood I slapped her rump with such force that she slithered right across the tiled floor and slammed into a cupboard – not my proudest moment, but it sobered her. The following morning she killed a starling in Kensington Gardens. Then she adopted my dotty mother whose brain was increasingly stricken with dementia, sharing her big chair most of the day as sweetly as a cavalier spaniel, but on the morning walk with me she was invariably a killer. Squirrels and small birds were her common victims, but she once disappeared down a burrow for forty desperately anxious minutes, at last emerging a hundred yards away with a big buck rabbit dead across her jaws; this I carried home and cooked for the dogs' dinner. My mother continued to call her Penny, seeming in her confusion to think her my devoted companion of 1945–60, but I could not bear to blur my recollection of so very different a dog and dubbed her Mrs Macbeth, seeing nothing of the Lady in her but a great deal of the wanton murderess.

She was a tough little thing, all too ready to challenge the geese and swans that towered over her in Kensington Gardens when my attention lapsed long enough for her to see them first, fearlessly belligerent towards Alsatians. The changing-rooms for bathers in the Serpentine were a constant attraction – what she did in them, having slipped through the railings that enclose them, I have no idea and she never returned with a trophy, but the yelps and screams of the women inside were audible a hundred yards away. In the time it took to walk the length of the enclosure, Mrs Macbeth could enter it, do her party trick, and be at the far end as I reached it, her timing always perfect.

A useful guardian of the house, with a proper bark rather than the yap so common to small dogs, the archetypal detester of postmen and the readers of gas meters, she had occasionally to be shut in my study rather than put them at risk, but I was not always sufficiently vigilant. One morning a motorcyclist delivered a National Gallery catalogue for which he required a signature, but had no pen and I had left mine on my desk; retrieving it gave Mrs Macbeth her opportunity to slip past me and launch an attack. It was a time when full-length one-piece black leathers were the fashionable garb of such young men and he was an exquisite example of the type, complete with black-visored black helmet and the codpiece effect of a prominent genital mount. I did not see the attack, but heard the yelp – his, not hers – and turned to see him bent low in pain, with Mrs Macbeth hanging from his loins, her teeth sunk into the codpiece. With some diplomacy I managed to detach her and, breathing heavily, the boy went on his way without threatening a lawsuit. In the late evening I was disturbed by something of a brawl immediately outside the house and, responding to evident cries of distress, I was fool enough to intervene. Providing distraction enough for the one man who was being thoroughly thumped by half-a-dozen others to escape, within seconds I found myself the object of their rage and in the scuffle was scraped along my garden wall like cheese against a grater. Escaping into the house I telephoned the police, removed my ruined shirt, sponged grit from my raw and bleeding back as best I could, and waited. And waited. A full hour later the bell rang and I opened the door to a solitary policeman who had come on foot, and let him in; he was no further than six feet into the hall when Mrs Macbeth, whom I had earlier settled with my mother for the night, suddenly appeared and seemed to launch herself from high on the stairs behind me like a *deus ex machina*, just when his hands were engaged in removing his helmet, to snap her jaws shut at precisely the point in his trousers where the motorcyclist boasted his codpiece. The brawl and the shredded flesh of my back seemed quite irrelevant as, for the second time that day, I had to deal with a young man doubled in agony, tears in his eyes, swearing like a trooper at a very small dog.

There were some four or five years of truculent behaviour, until it became evident that – as had been the case with my first Penny – she no longer relished the long morning walks.

Though she slept with my mother on the second floor she had always been alert to the brief preparations for them and had torn downstairs to add to Titian's urgings, but at fourteen or so she had increasingly often to be called, and at fifteen to be fetched. In her last year, at sixteen, a slow walk round the block was all that she wanted, and it was during one of these, in June 1993, as we turned the corner furthest from home, that she keeled over on the pavement. Seeing no evidence of breath in that tiny body, I seized her by the scruff of her neck, thumped her chest with my fist, felt her breathe again and rushed to Rusty's surgery. There, in the waiting-room, she died in my lap. 'A heart attack,' said Rusty, 'nothing to be done.' Wondering how I could tell my mother, whose dog she was far more than mine, I took her home, still warm, as though asleep. I climbed the stairs without her and, having broken the news, asked if she would like to see her and say farewell to the little animal who had adopted her – but was forced to recognise how deep was her descent into dementia. She stared at me without a glimmer of com-prehension and it was I who grieved for Mrs Macbeth, both valiant and vicious.

She had dominated Titian and was very much top dog until May 1988, when Mop (of whom much more anon) came to the house, a biggish bitch with something about her of both an Alsatian and a Karabaş (the Turkish sheepdog) and, at less than twelve months old (six of them in quarantine), utterly innocent of canine hierarchy. Mrs Macbeth tried a nip or two, but was nipped in return, and in response to my admonitions (more hugging and stern talking), slipped into neutrality. Titian's response to Mop should have been predict-able but took me by surprise – at first sight he fell in love with her, fierce physical love that he was too small to impose, slithering off her every time he attempted to mount her (though she was not on heat), ejaculating on her flanks with the frequency of which I had thought only the adolescent boy is capable. I have never seen a healthy dog so exhausted, and at the end of the day he could hardly stand without some sturdy piece of furniture on which to lean. Over two or three days he saw to her education – how to open doors with circular door-handles, standing on hind legs with a forepaw slightly inwards turned on either side of the handle, easing it round until the click of release is heard, then leaning backwards, pulling the door open in the inevitable fall; he taught her the rules of the house and let her take from him the chore of guarding it. At once inseparable, in Kensington Gardens he behaved with astonishing aplomb, seeming to introduce her, as might a young man his fiancée, not only to the few dogs with whom he had a friendly relationship, but to their owners. Walking with him at last became a pleasure without anxiety – except, perhaps, in autumn when, much the same colour as fallen leaves, he was often perfectly camouflaged.

Titian's attachment to the yellow velvet sofa was not one whit diminished by Mop's presence, nor was his custom of peeing on visitors' luggage; his interest in the theft of cheese, chicken and chocolate remained as strong, and I found him teaching Mop to stand erect and reach deep across a sideboard to slide a roast chicken within his shorter reach. She did not, however, share his uncontrollable enthusiasm for horses in Hyde Park and the warm dung in which he rolled so eagerly and ate with the relish of a coprophage. With Mop he became more tractable and obedient, and as never again did he run off on some tiresome purpose of his own, I learned to trust him – almost – and for the last five years of his life we were at peace. The death of Mrs Macbeth he took in his stride, but the final disappearance of the ever peripatetic Tom, the cat with whom he slept so often, caused him great anxiety. He was accustomed to Tom's shorter absences of two or three days, from which he returned with the bites and scratches of battle with other toms, but at four or five days Titian became dejected, restless and fretful, and for weeks whenever we walked round the block it seemed that he was watching and sniffing for a trace. I suppose that Tom's cock-o'-the-walk attitude to traffic had brought about his end.

In the summer of 1994 Titian seemed suddenly to age, weight falling away from him, his muzzle whitened. 'Perhaps he is older than we thought,' said Rusty, finding nothing wrong with him. In mid October, in hospital and very ill for a month, friends cared for the dogs. As I recovered, Titian grew worryingly frail and by mid November his greedy interest in food had faded to nothing. One morning, sitting on the small settee in the window, on which I always scribbled, I lifted him onto the other cushion so that I could, with a light touch, tell him how much I loved him, and he was responsive. 'I know,' I said to myself as much as to him, 'a chocolate biscuit might get you going again,' and went down to the kitchen to get one. At first he refused the quarter that I offered, but when I ate a quarter myself, he took it, with evident enjoyment, but would take no more, closed his eyes and slept, and while I poured scorn on the corruptions of the Turner Prize that year, his life deserted him. I did not feel him go. Again I grieved, again observing that the deaths of dogs grow more painful the more we experience them, but my grief and pain were as nothing compared with the grief and pain of Mop.

☙ 9 ☙

Mopsuestia, Mopsus, Mopsy, Mop

Mop I found in Turkey in September 1987. David George (distinguished photographer) and I were following the footsteps of Alexander the Great as he moved east and south across what used to be Asia Minor and had reached the rubble and wreckage of Mopsuestia, a ruined city supposedly founded by an ancient Greek seer named Mopsus, to the north of the site of the great battle of Issus. The climb was steep, sometimes on all fours, and our scrabbling was noisy, almost blotting out the whimper that I thought I had heard above and to the right; I heard it again, climbed towards it, and found a puppy half buried in a gully, her coat deeply snagged by the savage thorn bush in which she was hopelessly entangled. Urgently we snapped the branches of the bush, but when I lifted her free she screamed and it was then that I saw the damaged foreleg, broken below the shoulder, which was dislocated, and again above the paw; she was terribly dehydrated, her eyes glazed. I carried her, slithering down the hill to the first house we could see, and asked for water, but the man who brought it was the man who had thrown her away, and when I offered her the glass he dashed it from my hand.

In the village shop I hoped for milk and honey, but there was only yoghurt; this I poured into her mouth and she fell asleep. In a flea-ridden hotel in Osmaniye we were not allowed to take her to our room, but in the yard we found a wire cage in which she would be safe for the night, but before putting her in it, took the risk of manipulating her shoulder — there was no vet in the town and I could only guess which way to rotate it; to straighten the leg was easier — but the screams were terrible — and I set the breaks by containing the leg in rolls of newspaper held tight with the masking tape that I always carried to repair the holes in mosquito screens. Then she slept again. Later she ate the kebabs that should have been our dinner, slivers of cheese, more yoghurt and more water; in the morning, with tail-wagging relish, she experienced the pleasure of a Turkish breakfast — warm fresh bread, butter and honey. Her coat was running with fleas and blood-gorged ticks embedded in her ears and paws had to be twisted from her skin before we continued our journey to Issus. As she was too weak to walk and the splinted foreleg was a severe impediment, I emptied my knapsack of inessentials, topped the rest with my travelling pillow and put the pup on it, able to see the world, with her straight leg sticking out. This amused the Turks and on the fifth day one of them was gentle enough to let us take her to our room and she and I had a shower. She emerged a very pretty thing, her coat a greyish black, her paws the palest fawn. I was overwhelmed with anxiety, for I realised that when our duties to Alexander ended in a week or two, I would be compelled to leave her. Might it have been kinder to have broken her neck at Mopsuestia?

In Side, however, I had a friend, Osman Delikkulak, who introduced me to a German woman who had a walled garden and a huge gentle Alsatian, and she volunteered to care for the pup until arrangements could be made to get her to England; Osman also arranged the essential rabies injections; and within a month I returned to collect her and, as it were, to lose her for another six months as she languished in quarantine. Every Saturday I went to see her, taking cubes of cheese and chocolate and some garment – a T-shirt or underpants – in which I had slept, so that she could became accustomed to the odours of my body. I watched her grow; I watched her snout lengthen to suggest Alsatian ancestry, and her coat to take on the dense waterproof underfelt of the Turkish Karabaş – though she was not quite as big as either. Her puppy teeth fell out, she had her first heat, and she grew sway-backed with so much standing on her hind legs looking out for me, and at last, on 8 May 1988, I collected her from quarantine and took her home.

A quarantined dog has been in prison for six months, in solitary confinement, hearing, but never seeing, other dogs, its human contact a kennel maid who has sluiced its cell every day, changed its bedding (shredded newspaper in an aluminium tray), and brought it food and water, but never groomed or cuddled it. A quarantined dog has never walked further than the length and breadth of its quarters, has never run, has never experienced the intellectual benefit of such exercise. Such a dog as Mop, incarcerated as a puppy, knows nothing of comfort, of soft furniture and carpets, and the coordination required to climb stairs is as great a mystery as algebra and geometry. Mop, grown into a sizeable dog at ten months or so, had no real muscular development, no running skills and could not easily turn or stop, and the long staircase of the common London terrace house utterly defeated her – she fell up it as often as she tumbled down. When tired, she lay wherever she happened to be, seeming content with the hard wood floor or the cold tiles of the kitchen even when rug or carpet was within inches of her nose, and had to be persuaded onto the old settee that was specifically for dogs, set in the alcove where there was once a kitchen range. As for her sleeping on my bed – that was quite out of the question, for she had instinctively taken to guarding the house, sleeping across the front door or lying wakeful on a landing from which she could watch the lower windows and see or sense most comings and goings, inside and out, always prepared to growl, bare her teeth and bark with an urgent note until assured that all was well. Occasionally I could bribe her onto my bed, but when she thought me fast asleep, with the silent delicacy of the cat she'd slip away to do her duty by the door.

As she saw our relationship, she belonged to me and I to her; she had no affection for other people, rarely accepted food or treats from them, and occasionally expressed dislike by administering a nip to some accessible fat part of the body – usually the buttock but occasionally the waist or upper arm – never breaking skin or drawing blood, but pinching hard enough to let her victims know that they had incurred her displeasure. On the lead she was likely to object to any face that was not white and to moustaches, to children running noisily flat-footed to scare pigeons, to joggers running straight towards her, and to any fat person with what might be described as a funny walk; with all these I could feel an inaudible growl vibrating up the lead and knew that I must shorten it. Off the lead, the first sign of her misgiving was a series of short sharp exhalations through her nose – not quite a snort – followed by a hesitation in her gait and a lowering of hindquarters, as though about to leap, as once she did, at a very fat woman in a burqa, who fell backwards through a privet hedge. An Italian friend mistook her for a wolf and it is true that she grew to look a little lupine and in her playful moments seemed to call upon a lupine past, taking me for quarry. Her game with me was, as we walked in Kensington Gardens, to take my right hand in her mouth, very gently for a hundred yards or two, and then shift her grip to my wrist and up my forearm, increasing pressure until it almost hurt and I was far from upright; but the teeth bared by the hunting beast were as often bared in smiles, and there were nightly rituals of rolling on her back, grinning with pleasure, her eyes opened wide to show the whites.

For six months of the year she swam in the Round Pond, and for six months she did not; one day in April she left me with Titian and Mrs Macbeth (both of whom hated getting wet) and plunged into the Pond, ignoring the geese and ducks, swam parallel with the path on which we were, clambered out and rejoined us as though it were the most usual thing in the world; and one day in October she rolled in frost instead, and later, when it snowed, ran through this wonderful white stuff with her lower jaw open like a scoop.

In middle age Mop developed such gravitas that the *Daily Mail*, engaged in controversy with McDonald's over their beefburgers, asked to borrow her (with me as cicisbeo) to provide an illustration to an article with some such inflammatory headline as 'Not even a Dog will eat them'. As the branch in High Street Kensington refused to let us in – 'No dogs, no cameras' – beefburgers and other delicacies were bought to take away and the jape was performed on the pavement outside with the restaurant as backdrop. Mop behaved perfectly, sitting upright, turning her head to left and right in emphatic refusal even to sniff the wretched victuals, assuming such an expression of distress that only Greta Garbo and a vaselined lens could have matched it; a posse of staff came out to shoo us away, but by then the cameraman had a dozen shots to prove the point. There was then the problem of what to do with the rejected food and, knowing that Titian would not hesitate to gulp it down, I volunteered to take it home, but on the way – out of the limelight, so to speak – Mop ceased to be the fastidious canine gourmet and insistently demanded what she had earlier refused; it was with considerable relish that she consumed the mushy bun, the burger, limp gherkin and tomato paste, thrust her nose into a cup of chips leaving not a crumb, and on hind legs begged fervently for the chicken nuggets.

In 1994 I had the damaging first of several heart attacks. The front door ajar, I lay on the floor in the hall waiting for the ambulance with Mop and Titian surging anxiously about me, but so ferocious was their response when the paramedics arrived that they were too scared to come in. 'Call off your dogs,' they shouted through the gap, but by then I could not speak. A passing policeman saved the day; removing his tunic, he confronted Mop – the obvious top dog – as does a matador with cape and bull, and wrapping her head and forelegs in it when she sprang at him, pushed her backwards to the kitchen stairs and tossed her down them; Titian meekly followed. There were more heart attacks, much surgery and other unpleasant consequences; I began to have blackouts – a low blood pressure thing – for which nauseous preliminaries were warning enough that I must at once sit or lie in some comparatively safe place; when one happened in Kensington Gardens I made for the nearest tree and let Mop be my guardian until the episode passed, and I occasionally recovered to find curious passers-by standing fifty feet away, so fierce was her protective instinct.

It was between the first and second heart attacks that Titian died, and again I witnessed proof of canine emotion of a human kind. It seemed that nothing could assuage Mop's grief, her inconsolable misery more profound even than mine (and with fewer distractions), and for months, unresponsive to my comforting, she mourned, often refusing food, lacklustre on walks, indifferent to all my promptings. This ended, suddenly, on 2 March 1995, when on impulse but not whim – for she was far from my kind of dog – I collected from the Mayhew Animal Home in Kensal Green, a blonde and silky little bitch with a pretty face and bushy tail (the extraordinarily long hairs of which I sometimes, as a joke, wore on the collar of my overcoat), in desperate need of a new home after three years and as many pregnancies as the plaything of an Alsatian guard dog. Immediately she triggered all Mop's dormant maternal responses and, over-whelmingly mothered, was in no time house-trained, sharing duties as guardian, and walking demurely on the lead. Nusch (named so after the wife of a Surrealist French poet, Paul Éluard, because it is such a sweet pillow-talking sound) became the clown in contrast to Mop's gravity, the seductress, the warm, effusive, wriggling, nuzzling, dance-on-my-hind-legs-and-tickle-my-tummy dog.

My heart condition worsened; the second attack pre-cipitated a quadruple bypass and such a poor recovery that I could no longer live in a tall narrow house of rooms tied together by steep stairs. Seeking one in which I could more or less manage with one floor and a garden, I found it in Wimbledon, and the vast extent of the Common with its ponds, heathered heathland and great forest trees, replaced Kensington Gardens. Mop, now twelve, seemed not much interested in the new house; I watched her inspect it, slowly and diligently, and I'd swear that she thought it had too many doors – the front door, the side door, the back door, a conservatory door and a French window in the small room that I chose to make my bedroom; and as for the windows through which, in Eldon Road, she could see the street and form an opinion of the passers-by, through these in Wimbledon there was no high vantage point from the stairs, and to see through them at all she must stand on her hind legs. It was clear that she no longer wished to be the guardian of my house and surrendered the responsibility to busy little Nusch who clearly thought that this made her top dog, but when she nipped Mop to indicate her new authority, she was very firmly put in her place. I complicated these matters of hierarchy by bringing a young Alsatian bitch into the house – Winckelmann, soon abbreviated to Winck (though J. J., Winckelmann's initials, would have been an easier abbreviation for non-German speakers to master); this seemed not at all to bother Mop, but upset Nusch, who was far too small to impose her will on so boisterous and big a newcomer. Even so, the three of them settled well enough, and Mop, at last, decided that she would sleep on my bed – oh the joy of reaching out in the middle of the night to run my fingers through the dense fur about her neck, to feel her silken ears, to hold a beautiful forepaw . . .

On the first day of November 2001 men came to plant an oak tree – not a spindly sapling from a garden centre, but a young forest tree, delivered by a crane, intended as a monument for all the old dogs in my life whose bones, bared by earlier burials and by the wind and rain to which they were exposed on the flat roof of the old house, I had brought with me – that was every dog but Prince, washed away by the tide at Whitstable as we waited to go to war with Germany, and Penny, at peace in my mother's garden in Castle Hedingham for more than forty years. They dug the hole and tenderly I laid the bones that seemed so fine and fragile compared with the remembered flesh, and then the skulls, Titian's broad, Hecate's tiny, Trollop's big, those of Susie and her progeny less easy to distinguish – and then a scattering of earth and the tears that were the flood of memory. The men gave me a little time before they lowered the bole of the tree, and there it stood, fine and straight, while they filled the narrow crack around it, stamping hard enough to wake the dead whom I would have been so glad to see again.

Six days on, on 7 November 2001, Mop died. Exactly, to the very day, fourteen years before, in 1987, we had landed at Heathrow and she had begun her quarantine – it did not, I think, obliterate her origin, for whenever I returned from subsequent journeys in Turkey, she showed concentrated interest in my shoes, the bottoms of my trousers and, of course, the knapsack in which she had been carried for five hundred miles and more.

It was, as dogs' deaths go, merciful. We walked on the Common on Sunday, exploring further than usual, and she had been very much her bright-eyed jaunty self until, suddenly, she played her extraordinary trick of deciding to go home, drawing a bead on where we had left the car, and launching herself in a straight line to it, negotiating brambles, nettles, ferns and tangled undergrowth, lolloping through puddles and scrambling over fallen trunks, with me, Nusch and Winckelmann (particularly Nusch in her silken coat) struggling to keep pace with her. She was invariably right; the car was always where she said it was. At one point a huge prone trunk defeated her and she slid backwards from it; I laughed – but I shall never forget the look she gave me. In the evening she would eat no dinner; never a greedy dog, a fast her occasional custom, this was not a reason for anxiety, but by Monday evening other signs were evident. In my experience old dogs decide to die though nothing is amiss with them, no cancer, no failure of liver or kidneys, no diabetes – it is just that the time has come. Dogs shut down their systems; they refuse food first, then water, then wait for coma to set in, but with a strong dog the wait is not easy, not without pain, and when consciousness becomes murky, the benign vet should do his deed.

Mop, in whose ear I had so often murmured when wrestling with her, 'You're a big strong dog,' was not strong in the end and, with overwhelming relaxation of her will, she faded very fast, seemingly without pain; for a while she responded to my touch with a twitch of the tail, and let me carry her into the garden, but towards the end I did not move her and her only response to my touch was a slight widening of her eyes. I watched her throughout the Tuesday, sinking, at the foot of my bed; at 2.30 in the night I stroked her, her breathing quiet and steady, but when I reached for a paw two hours later, it was cold. The rest of her was warm under my cardigan, but I could hear nothing, could feel no breath on my cheek and, in spite of the warmth, knew that she had gone. How cussed of her, I thought, to wait until after I had buried Titian, her lover and friend, with whom she ought to be; I shall have to get another tree.

'A Sequoia Sempervirens,' said the tree man, gazing skyward, 'will look just splendid in two hundred years.' 'I shan't be here,' I murmured, and chose a more modest black pine; and under it she lies, wrapped in my cardigan, with cubes of chocolate and cheese as grave goods, the gifts that I had taken her every week in her half year in quarantine. It was a heavy business in the wind and rain, lightened only by one thing – somehow one of Titian's jawbones had caught in the wicker basket in which all the old bones were treasured, somehow something made me open it, and so one small relic of the friend for whom she had grieved so long was buried with her.

Why should a comparatively sane man be so stricken by the death of a dog as to make a ceremony and a memorial of it? Mop was a pup worth less than nothing to a Turkish peasant, a pup whose neck would have been broken with a rabbit chop by a kindly passer-by, an affront to the breeders for whom Cruft's is Elysium. I can only answer that between us there was an understanding that did not much depend on any conventional means of communication between man and dog, the bark and the command; in my relationship with her I sensed, not mawkish sentiment, but something beyond scientific recognition, almost lost, but natural and ancient beyond the numbering of years. The dog was, perhaps, the primary tool of man when he first raised himself on his hind legs, older than any sounds that we might recognise as language.

Friends said of Mop, 'You gave her a good life,' as though this might be some consolation for her death; indeed I did, but she gave me a good life too and were our exchanged lives placed in a balance, her gift, I am certain, would weigh heavier and prove to have been the more generously given. She kept one thing only for herself, the fine-mannered dignity that is occasionally to be discerned in dogs. Byron saw it in his Newfoundland and I have no better words for Mop – 'Beauty without vanity, strength without violence, courage without ferocity, and all the virtues of man, without his vices.' Byron would have understood my proud claim that Mop was the only dog in England to have roamed the battlefield of Issus where, in 333 BC, the history of the world abruptly changed in an unlikely victory of his beloved Greeks over the confounded Persians; she was in the knapsack on my back as we gazed at the stars one night, knowing that we had not found the site; and she was there again next morning when David George and I, with ancient classical accounts in hand, climbed the huge mound on which stands the castle of Toprakkale, upset a roosting eagle, and saw, spread before us in relief, the site, exactly as described two thousand years before.

10

Nusch

What can I say of Nusch, the infuriatingly feminine mongrel whom I never loved enough? On Titian's death I had hoped to find a big bitch at the Mayhew Animal Home, smooth and brown like Susie long ago, with a resonant deep bark and an air of gravity; instead, I found one with voluminous fluffy knickers and an even fluffier tail, a yapping bark that tore my eardrums, and no gravity at all, but she was in a bad way and needed to be found. Aged three or so, she had been dumped at the Mayhew pregnant, had born eight pups who at eight weeks were almost as large as she, and was exhausted, skinny and inclined to be both fearful and snappy with strangers; there were happy applicants for all eight pups, but no one wanted her. Often, over the years, I shook my head at her and said, 'You are not the dog I wanted,' and she, catching my meaning, had hangdog slunk away. But she was mine for nearly thirteen years and I grew accustomed to her presence, her soft plumpness and the long golden hairs on my clothes that sometimes led to my being mistaken for a man who had a human rather than a canine mistress. She had a double – in Naples; we met in the Piazza del Plebiscito, but her mistress mistook me for a man of evil intention and hurried her away.

On 19 March 1995, her farewells at the Mayhew done (and it was clear that she had everyone there in thrall), I took her to the car, and there she scrabbled her way into the foot-well of the front passenger seat and did her best to hide. We went at once to Kensington Gardens, but there she was overcome with agoraphobia and, trembling, buried her head between my knees, making it impossible to walk. I laughed – quite the wrong thing to do – and tried manhandling her but she would not be steered; nor would she look about her, but hung her head and looked only at the ground. Then we went home and Mop took charge of her – and so did I, in taking her to bed. The following morning we again attempted the Gardens; she was hesitant at first but Mop persuaded her to venture a few yards away and then to run – and again I witnessed, as I had with Mop, the phenomenon of inability to stop in a dog who had never before been able to run far or fast, a dog who could halt only by crashing into something, in this case one of the big chicken-wire 'bins' in which dead leaves were then collected. Very quickly she learned how to slow her pace, twist, turn and stop, and very quickly too she learned to coordinate her feet on stairs, to be civil to other dogs – make friends, indeed – and lose her fear of strangers, to chase squirrels and pigeons (but not geese and ducks), and to roll on and in horse dung and anything else that stank. She was not much interested in water and never swam, but would stand in two inches of it, barking hysterically, while Mop or Winck retrieved thrown sticks.

Food was her obsession. I think she had had, if not to fight for every scrap, certainly to be very quick about it. From the very first in my company she gulped her rations down and then snatched food from Mop who, sweet natured, often looking at me with what in human behaviour would have been a wan smile and a shrug, let her have it; this meant that Mop, always slow and delicate with food, had to be guarded until her dish was empty if she was not to starve and Nusch be as fat as a balloon. Greed – not quite the word, for this behaviour was bred of years of hunger and anxiety – and the high-pitched bark that obliterated every other sound, were her only flaws, and I loved her as best I could, but it was more fondness and loyalty than love, for she was just not my kind of dog.

For four years Mop's protégé, she changed when we moved to Wimbledon on St Valentine's Day in 1999. In the first week she began to take on the guardianship of the house and, particularly, the garden, encountering foxes for the first time, who insouciantly leaped onto the garden walls to roost in the intertwining knots of ivy, out of reach, mocking her. She wore habitual paths across the grass in their pursuit, and tunnels through the shrubs massed against the walls; and while Nusch was busy, busy, busy, Mop warned them off with a deep bark or two, and then at an ambling pace, explored, pausing to greet with a nudge of her wet nose the several families of toads that had long been in residence, or pointed to fledglings as yet incapable of flight, cowering in the undergrowth. Mop brought her intellect to bear on the smells and traces of the night's visitors, analysing and registering – and that, at least as much as exercise, is for the thinking dog, the purpose of the daily walk. Nusch just dashed about being territorial, yet always outwitted by the foxes.

One influential reason for buying the house was its walled garden, once an orchard and wonderfully extensive for a London suburb, large enough for the dogs to exercise themselves if I were ever unable to walk with them – but it had no gates. While these were being made, the gap was closed with a frame of netting, secure enough, I thought, but I was wrong, for Nusch, still very slim and supple, whom until then I had thought timorous, had gained courage with her new territorial responsibilities, wriggled under the frame and set off to explore the neighbourhood. Of this I knew nothing until the police telephoned to say that she was at the local station. She had crossed roads and found her way the long mile to the famous tennis courts (fortunately out of season), there to be arrested as a lost dog. I was surprised (but relieved) that she had allowed herself to be picked up by a stranger, and deeply grateful that she had been spotted by a benevolent constable.

Her next adventure was on one of the wilder parts of the Common – wilder by far than the flat and ordered expanse of Kensington Gardens – where, framed by wooded banks, long and steep, lies the pond into which Susie had jumped, breaking the ice, on Christmas Day a quarter of a century before. In the warmth of early summer the water was densely covered with a bright green floating weed that Nusch, leaping over fallen tree trunks, storming down the bank at speed, took for firm ground and was in and under it before I could curb her with a shout. She was not in danger and scrambled out without my help, but was so decked in the weed about her head and shoulders that she resembled a ridiculous painting of *Ondine*, a water sprite, by Agasse, in the Musée d'Art in Geneva – and I laughed.

I know that dogs have a sense of humour and that some even go through the motions of laughter (though omitting its sound), but I should also have known by then that dogs do not much like being laughed *at*, that Nusch was particularly wounded if I laughed at her, and that no amount of cuddling and comforting was ever quite enough to wipe away the insult. When she dislocated her right knee, Onno Wieringa, who had taken over Rusty's surgery on his retirement (it took me years to abandon so reliable a vet for one in Wimbledon), shaved the entire leg, revealing a soft white skin so different, so strange, so odd without the fluffy knockers, and as he led her, still wobbly with anaesthetic, from his operating quarters, again I laughed – and for that thoughtless cruelty I have never forgiven myself. I did not laugh when, lying in the sun, her naked leg exposed to it, she was badly sunburned.

My last laugh, hysterical, nervous, helpless, was caused by Nusch, but she was not its object. Disturbing a heron just as it had taken a sizeable goldfish from my pond, the beautiful bird dropped it and flew off, the broken-backed fish floundering helplessly in the water. I swear that it looked me straight in the eye and I did what I felt compelled to do – hoicked it out and killed it. Then, feeling that I had some responsibility for the corpse, I dug a hole deep enough to frustrate the foxes and buried it. Of this I thought no more until, weeks later, invited to lunch with Prince Michael of Kent, I let the dogs into the garden for ten minutes before setting off for our rendezvous in the Polish Club, South Kensington. I do not customarily lunch with princes; I doubt if I know how to behave in exalted company; I was anxious about the informality of my clothes, for spring moth had dined on my only suit; and I did not want to be late. But late I was. I called the dogs. They did not come. I went in search of them and found that Nusch, filthy with earth, had retrieved the goldfish from its grave and that she and Winck were rolling on its mouldering shreds of flesh. One disintegrating fish no bigger than a sprat releases a volume of vile and clinging stink out of all proportion to its body. If I returned the dogs to the house every room would be uninhabitable, but I could not leave them in the garden. I had time, I thought, to bathe them. Stripped to my under-pants, I soaped and hosed them, but when dry, the stink was as strong as ever; I soaped and hosed again and still the stink clung to their coats – but this had to be enough. I hauled on my clothes and rushed off to meet the prince, aware throughout my journey on the Underground that I could still smell the stink; was it on my flesh, my clothes, or only in my nostrils? The mutual friend who was our host occasionally reminds me that my first words to the prince were 'Oh, how do you do – do I stink of fish?'

Another friend, an historian and shrewd observer, recalls that on her first visit to the house I bade her sit on the sofa while I made tea, and there Nusch joined her, striking a deliberately beautiful pose as appealing and pathetic as any painted by Landseer. She placed her forepaws in Pamela's lap, let her body settle into a serpentine line that ran elegantly the length of her body from nose to tail, gazed directly into her eyes and, stock still, held the pose until I returned. 'I seem to have made a friend,' said Pamela, disconcerted by the pleading intensity of this behaviour so far from ordinary canine friendliness. To this I, apparently insouciant, replied, 'Oh, she'll do anything to make me jealous,' and poured the tea. Pamela was, of course, quite right and far from the first, or last, visitor to be enlisted in Nusch's doomed stratagem to provoke my sense of possession to make me love her more.

In Mop's last few months in 2002 Nusch became aggressive to her in a premature attempt to become top dog, but the old bitch simply did not care and always turned away. With Mop's death she turned her aggression on Winck, but she too did not care and throughout her life had no sense at all of top-doggery. Poor Nusch – attempting coups when their objects, both much larger than she, did not care a hoot for her political juggling. She seemed not to miss Mop, but when, in 2005, Jack, a very damaged whippet, was wished on me by the Mayhew, she behaved, if not with quite the motherliness that Mop had given her, warmly enough, even to the extent of letting Jack share the comfortable, sagging old leather chair from which dogs watch me at my typewriter. In due course she grew plump, decided that she felt the cold and, ducking under the duvet at my feet, discreetly moved north to snuggle in my arms. Her hearing deserted her – almost a blessing, for it meant that she was no longer troubled by fireworks (exploded in Wimbledon for the most trivial occasions) – and cataracts dimmed her sight; if she ran into the woods on the Common I had to hurry after her, knowing that when she failed (as she always did) to catch the quarry that she chased, she would be bewildered and distressed.

At last, at fifteen or sixteen (how can one know the age of a second-hand dog?) she decided that she had had enough of life and began to do what some of her predecessors had done: Titian and Mop quite suddenly refused to eat or drink, fell quickly into coma and quietly faded away. Nusch just refused to eat. Six weeks of toing and froing to the vet revealed nothing physically amiss. Drugs failed to stimulate her appetite, but I clung to hope because she continued to drink. Once in a while she took a sliver of food no larger than a postage stamp, but this she did to please me rather than herself, for her response to such old temptations as tinned sardines and Parma ham, blue cheese and white chocolate was almost always to turn her head away as though these were quite disgusting. Then for ten days, still drinking, she ate nothing, not a morsel, and instead of snoozing her life away, she stood for hours on end, head down, tremors running through her body. I thought of Elizabeth I standing for fifteen hours before her death.

On 23 November 2007 I put her on my bed and lay

encircling her, waiting for the vet. I could not ask Onno Wieringa to come so far and turned to a local man; while he sheared the hair on a foreleg to find a vein Nusch raised her head and pressed against my cheek. The first thrust of the needle made her scream with pain and at that I almost stopped him, but cold sanity drove me on and as the poison ran into her vein I sensed her go. I felt a terrible responsibility for killing her. Days later, tidying my rooms for the daily woman who came to clean them once a week, I found the tiny tuft of silken hair, golden, soft and featherweight, shorn for the needle – remember me, remember me, it said, and the memories it conjured were unbearable.

Nusch lies now as near to her old companion, Mop, as I dared dig the hole; always in her shadow, in death she lies in the shadow of her tree.

⚜ 11 ⚜

Winckelmann, Winck

Winck and Jack mourned the death of Nusch. 'Absurd,' the sane man comments, 'we expect better of you than such silly sentimental anthropomorphism' – but it was true, their mood was uncharacteristically restrained, their playfulness departed, and they did not bark. Winck had a deep-chested woof, Jack a weird high-pitched croak hinting at hysteria, but I heard neither for two months or so and was discomforted by their silence. I mimicked Jack but she did not respond – Winck was too low a baritone for mimicry; neither the barks of other dogs nor the eerie cry of foxes triggered a response, and even the arrival of herons to plunder the pond of dormant frogs went unremarked. I dare say that they found some comfort in each other's company and I know that they assuaged my grief.

I have the BBC to thank for Winck's arrival in the house. On the Tuesday of Easter Week, 2000, someone in that much more loathed than loved institution, prompted to make a programme about the good done by the Mayhew Home, asked me to go there and suckle tiny puppies taken far too early from their dam and dumped in a cardboard box. This done, I wandered off to see what dogs might be loose in the outside enclosure and saw among the twenty or so what I took to be an Alsatian puppy. She saw me too, and as I walked past, followed my passage with a slow turn of her head, her stare unblinking. Beyond, on the patch of grass that was once a garden, lay a sad old dog, too old, too big, too obviously frail to be adopted, and I sat with him for some minutes, gently teasing his ears, before, in melancholy mood, rejecting the notion that I should perhaps volunteer to take him on, I walked back past the Alsatian pup. She had not moved since our earlier encounter, nor did she move with this, but again fixed her eyes on me with the same absolute concentration, turning her head to match my pace. I have ever since maintained that this was indeed a case of love at first sight 'across a crowded room'.

St Francis of Assisi (unofficially the patron saint of all living creatures) must have been on her side, performing a small miracle, for what I had seen behind the wire was quiet, doleful and definitely a puppy small enough to cuddle. I did what more had to be done for the BBC and went home – and the puppy came to mind. She lurked there throughout Wednesday, wrecking my concentration on other matters. On Maundy Thursday friends enquired the reason for my sombre mood and I confessed. 'Go for it,' they said, and in some anguish I answered 'I can't – Mop will be upset.' Mop, then almost thirteen, and I, had a strange and strong possession of each other, and I had determined not to have another dog before her death, so greatly did I value this fierce tenderness, but 'Go for it,' they said again, 'Mop will come round to her.' And so it was that on Good Friday I collected her and brought her home to Wimbledon.

But – and this is where St Francis played his part – what I collected was not the cuddly puppy some four or five months old that I thought I had seen, but an adolescent of a year or so, more or less fully grown, puppyish and puppy plump, but four feet long from the point of her nose to the root of her tail, with eighteen inches more of that with which to sweep things from low tables. I could not believe that I had been so mistaken, but I was and remained utterly seduced by the eyes, the ears, the teeth and the ecstatic wild demeanour of which there had not been the slightest hint when I first saw her. We paused for a walk on the Common where a friend was to meet us with Mop and Nusch, and Winck, on the lead, launched into a run that I could not halt, so strong was she, and to any educated onlooker we must have resembled a nonsense drawing by Edward Lear. She slowed when, at last, we encountered Mop, and their greeting done, we wandered off to the heart of the Common and I risked letting her off the lead. She ran like an arrow for a hundred yards, stopped, turned round, ran back – and I'd swear that for the rest of her life she was never more than twenty or thirty yards away from me.

At home she began by crunching, irreparably, my glasses, though they were guaranteed to withstand the tread of an elephant. Within a week she ate an irreplaceable book on the design of motor cars, the Arts Council's most recent set of accounts, and what I assumed to have been a delicious cherry pie made by the local baker, foolishly left on the kitchen table. Within a month she nipped through a dozen mahogany curtain rings waiting for new curtains to be delivered, chewed the underfelt of two carpets, mauled a roll of exquisite velvet inherited from my mother (who had never found a use for it), pulled down and gnawed one of the blinds in my study, beheaded all but one of the peonies in the garden and trampled flat an extravagant and exotic purchase from the National Trust nurseries at Wisley.

When someone at the Mayhew telephoned to ask how we were getting on – 'Fine,' I said, 'but why do you ask?' 'Oh,' came the answer, 'we thought she might have behavioural problems.' 'No, no – it is I who have those,' I replied, glancing through my study window to see her wrestling with the hosepipe as though she were the infant Hercules strangling serpents.

Naming her took more than a moment's thought. Her previous owners, Indians who had expected her to be a guard dog for their curry restaurant, had called her Tigriss, which would not do – she was not the least catlike, and even if I docked the erroneous second S, I saw no point in naming her after a river. Friends assisted in my musing: 'What about Winckelmann?' suggested one of them. 'Wasn't he the son of a German shepherd?' And that was that – she was christened Winckelmann, the W pronounced as a V, swiftly shortened to Winck, the sound short, sharp, emphatic and ideal for calling. Within hours she answered to it – but then she was a bright girl and had already learned something of every dog's command of English, and the meaning of emphatic gesture. Poor Nusch at first ran whimpering into corners if I raised my hand to scratch my head, but Winck had no such fears, only a wonderful self-confidence, and late in life, when deaf but still clear-sighted, knew exactly what my gestures meant.

Winckelmann, a great early art historian, was, of course, not the son of a shepherd but a shoemaker – Winck was a destroyer of shoes. She had the noble head of the Alsatian, the huge ears pricked, the brown eyes warm and honest. Her legs were stout and strong, her paws as big as a child's hand, and at walking pace she affected the bearing of a catwalk model, swinging her hips in preposterous seduction; at speed this gait straightened out and I could see the working dog in her, determined, purposeful, instinctive, cooperative, the ancient hunter to my gatherer. Nusch played with her until exhausted, racing, chasing, tussling over sticks, their relationship swiftly so very close that I wondered if her earlier companion as a yard dog had been an Alsatian too. Mop tolerated but disciplined her in the matter of access to my bedroom – 'This is my territory,' she said with nips and growls; even so, in the early morning, Winck used to creep in, silent as a kitten and, if Mop was not still there to warn her off with a low grumble in her throat, climbed onto my bed and lay beside me, dovetailed, her head on the other pillow. Winck immediately had the makings of a great dog and would, I knew, gentle the grief when Mop died in a year or two, as I knew she must, though I could hardly bear the thought of it. Kipling put it too coolly with his, 'Brothers and sisters, I bid you beware of giving your heart to a dog to tear.'

That warning I can paraphrase as, 'I bid you beware of giving your books to a dog to tear.' It was not that I gave the books to Winck – she took them, and some weeks passed before I caught her in the act. At first I did not know which dog was the miscreant, only that she destroyed old books that were rare and irreplaceable, though of interest only to an art historian, and then one day, not sitting at my desk but quietly reading in a chair and not immediately visible, into my study came Winck. She sniffed a shelf and, having found a volume from the days when animal glue was used in binding books, she turned her head on one side and delicately removed it with her front teeth gripping the spine. There the delicacy ended in the sound of cloth rent and paper shredded until the glue was exposed and, lying on her tummy with the ruined book between her forepaws, she could savour what a century before could as easily have been cow-heel jelly as the binder's glue.

Sleeping with Dogs

At seven stone when she first came, she was big and boisterous in her affection. When Miss Mabel, Diana Rigg's Jack Russell bitch, came to stay instead of going into kennels, she and Winck went mad with pleasure, racing hither and yon, she small enough to run under Winck as though she were a bridge. In their first chase Winck collided with the back of my knees and felled me like a log – and there I lay, helpless with laughter, flat on my back at Diana's feet, where perhaps all men should be.

With Winck's coming I was reminded that three is the perfect number of dogs, enough to be a self-regulating society among themselves without usurping my place as top dog – and life settled down to a routine in which they depended on me only for food and the long walks on the Common. A friend gave Winck a football and in no time she was dribbling it expertly between her forepaws until Mop tried to take it from her – then she seized it in her teeth and punctured it; half-a-dozen footballs later I decided that we must find a longer-lasting toy. When Miss Mabel was still with us men came to dig a pond, eight feet deep and fifty long, and she and Winck drank their tea and ate their sandwiches, and when the great hole was ready to be filled, they could not be kept out of it – though when it was full and the ducks and herons came to inspect it, and newts and frogs, dragonflies, leeches, snails and water-boatmen all appeared from nowhere as though to reinforce the tales of Creation as told in Genesis, Winck never again set foot in it; Miss Mabel, of course, returned to Diana.

Winck matured into a grave and beautifully mannered guardian and friend. Big, she looked sufficiently formidable for owners of small dogs to steer them away from her and even pick them up, but once her joyful madcap adolescence was over, there was no gentler, safer dog on the Common and, entirely without savagery (though I dare say that she might have come to my defence), no other dog had anything to fear from her. Mop's death she marked, less with her own grief than her acknowledgement of mine, taking her place in my bedroom; this was not in any sense triumphalism, but recognition of my misery, which was acute; on my bed she did not push against me as Susie had, seeming to absorb my physical pain, but simply lay beside me, responding only if I reached out to run my fingers through her coat. 'When will you replace Mop?' friends were fool enough to ask when three months had passed. 'Replace?' I responded. 'Replace that touch, that sound, that presence, that determined character? I could no more replace any dog than I could replace my mother. If God wants me to have another, he will see to it.' I fancy that, for me, proof of the existence of God and his heaven will be my waking one morning to find all my old dogs sleeping on my bed or nuzzling my face and demanding to be let into the garden – then I shall know that I am dead, in heaven, and utterly wrong in my agnosticism.

For all my conviction that the sane man should have three dogs, the expected three months of grieving for Mop extended to three years, and then, just before New Year 2005, the call came. 'It's James, from the Mayhew,' said the voice, 'we've got a whippet bitch – are you interested?' James will be amused to know that his, for the moment, was the voice of God. Winck accepted Jack at once; there was neither a particular enthusiasm nor the slightest sign of antipathy – just very gentle acceptance. Jointly affected when Nusch died, I found them more often sleeping together on my bed for comfort in their mourning. Did they, like me, sense her presence still, in odd movements seen only in the corner of my eye and in odd sounds that only I could hear, her name tripping too readily from my lips when calling Winck and Jack the whippet?

I was determined to get my new Nusch from the Mayhew, but a friend took me, willy-nilly, to an Animal Centre run by the RSPCA principally for young dogs that are discarded toys, dogs that have been bruised, battered and burned and are held as evidence against their former owners, and a more motley lot waiting for pity. I wept for the sad old bitch with only a year or two of life in her, and for the tiny pup, the mismatch of Chihuahua and Jack Russell, so isolated from her kind and from human warmth that she could never learn to be a proper dog. I longed to take home the tall Alsatian cross, eight months old, leaping and bounding against the wire mesh, but knew that I no longer had the strength to be companionable to so magnificent a creature. But oh how she barked – a resonant base bark, a Fyodor Chaliapin of barks, a Boris Christoff bark, a beautiful bark that would, I was certain, restore the barks of Winck and Jack.

December, January and February passed, and then, at last, I felt tough enough to fill the gap and on 8 March 2008 took Winck with me to see what we could find at the Mayhew. I fell for a handsome pale brown bitch tall enough for my hand to rest on her collar, but bigger than Winck and wildly obstreperous. Winck clearly disagreed and I could see her point. All but one of the other nineteen bitches she ignored, lying by my chair, but for one she rose to her feet and exchanged the most gentle of greetings; thus it was that we settled on the ugliest and most pathetic-seeming mutt, the sort of dog from which many recoil in fear, the sort that ends its days for ever unwanted and unloved. 'She was Winck's choice,' I said to all who raised an eyebrow – and indeed she was, and there was never a cross word between them. I named her Lottie, eschewing the correct German form, Lotte, because I'd had trouble enough with Winckelmann.

Lottie, largely ignored by Winck who was already pursuing the business of growing old gracefully, took a long year to settle down, her overwhelmingly sobering experience the unexpected death of Jack the whippet in July 2009, leaving a gap impossible to fill, though one of its consequences was the oddly untroubled serenity of all our lives until the spring of 2012. There is much to be said for the relationship of an old dog and an old man, its custom, composure and tranquillity, though the old man knows how fragile it is when both are stalked by death. Winck's occasional inclination to chase and play quite gone, her long walks on the Common much more an intellectual exercise than physical, her slow meanderings in the garden often activity enough, she seemed quietly content. Her increasing deafness did not much trouble her, though we touched each other more; but, as with so many Alsatians, her hind legs weakened and I had often to help her onto my bed. Early in April 2012 she had her last walk on the Common, she with her wobbly legs, me on my crutches, and without the often disorderly company of Lottie – and I had a premonition that it would be the last. On familiar territory, it was not a long walk in terms of distance, but we were plodding for more than an hour and she was exhausted by it; the last few hundred yards were tough for her, and slow, but it was warm and bright, trees were in bud and blossom, and it was a fine day to say farewell to the Common.

A week or so later, on a Saturday, just as I and a friend had finished a kitchen lunch and were reading a *Guardian* between us, with Winck not quite under the table in readiness for titbits, she keeled over onto her side, shaking violently. At once I was on my knees holding the beautiful head that otherwise would bang on the cold tiles, until the tremors stilled. Then, limp and seeming paralysed, her eyes were the only sign of life. I telephoned the vet's emergency number. 'Bring her in,' said the secretarial voice that then told me exactly what the exorbitant fee would be, as though to deter me. 'I can't. She is too heavy to lift. She is dying and I want her to die here, at home.' 'We don't do visits at weekends,' said the voice, 'you must bring her in.' With 'I can't' the conversation ended and, as things turned out, I was to be hugely relieved that the voice had been so inconsiderately intransigent.

I found a waterproof sheet, an eiderdown, small soft cushions, constructed a nest for her on the floor of my study and, together, we half carried, half dragged, her to it. By then she had vomited and emptied both bowels and bladder; apart from her open eyes and almost imperceptible breathing, she seemed as good as dead and I was, as it were, determined that she should die in comfort and my presence. She did not. For eight hours I sat with her, and then there was movement – not much, but enough to suggest that the crisis might be over. For three days the vigil lasted as some feeble strength returned, and, at last, a very unsteady and bewildered Winck could be clumsily supported into the garden. Further recovery was slow, but a treasured reward for the effort – even if it meant getting up in the early hours to go into the garden with her to empty what had become a bladder of much reduced capacity, inclined to spontaneous emptying if not stimulated every three hours day and night. This was a small price to pay for her continued company, and no great effort, for the pains sparked by my crumbling spine were as effective in waking me as any alarm clock, and over a weekend in November she had a less dramatic episode, but was again paralysed. The nest had to be reconstructed in my study. She drank very little, ate nothing, and had frequently to be re-positioned to prevent cramp. By the Monday it was clear that she was dying, but death was unkind and stayed away. On Wednesday 26 November 2012 I called Roger Bralow, and he, with infinite sympathy, gently found a vein and put an end to her. I held her in my arms; he quietly slipped away without a word; I howled.

Wrapped in the beloved black silk jacket that I wore on the pilgrimage to Santiago de Compostela, she rests in the stone sarcophagus made for her three years before by the sculptor Nicholas Moreton, joining Jack, who was first to occupy it; it is inscribed with the one word DOMINICANES, a Renaissance pun on the Dominican Order (the Dogs of God). So late in the year there were few flowers in the garden, but I and the friend who loved her as much as I and saw me through this crisis found among them the last rose and first camellia, the perfumed leaves of bay, sprigs of lavender, sage, thyme and, of course, rosemary, and on a bed of these we sweetened her departure.

Giacometti, Jack

Of Jack the first word that I had was in the doldrum days at the very end of December 2004. Found in the very nick of time – though the Mayhew's vets were not then quite sure of that – she had been thrown over a high wall into the yard of a disused industrial building into which no one ever went, though fortunately someone did. Without shelter, food or water, her only comfort windblown dead leaves, she had starved for so long that she was little more than alive and might not recover. If she did, she would need to go to someone who had the time and knowledge to continue the regime of care and, if possible, be with other dogs, for she seemed either to have forgotten or never to have known what it is to be a dog, unresponsive to any stimulus. 'What colour is she?' I asked, and I swear that I was given the answer, 'Blue.' That did it – another Hecate – and from then on I thought of her as mine.

With nursing at the Mayhew she put on weight; when she was down to four feeds a day on 15 January 2005 they let me take her. Nusch went with me; old, plump, soft and cuddly, but occasionally inclined to grumble, I took her so that she could, as it were, discover Jack for herself and bring her home, rather than be presented with an unfamiliar intruder on her territory. The trick worked – but then it always does. In Winck's reaction I had absolute trust for she was incapable of jealousy. Yet again I witnessed the maternal instinct of bitches switched into action by the vulnerability of another animal. Jack, however, was utterly unresponsive, not fearful, but merely without reaction to gestures of affection or interest from either the dogs or me.

She was still so painfully thin that, standing against the light, I could see through her limbs, the bones as clear as in an X-ray, and neither fat nor flesh lay between her thin skin and her ribs and spine and hips. She trembled – as whippets often do – and, standing still, hung her head as though interested in nothing. She ate uneasily the small handfuls of food I gave her four or five times a day, her head so low over it that it was almost as upside-down as a flamingo's; between these snacks she slept, nothing else rousing her to activity. She seemed to find some small comfort in Nusch, but was at first in fear of Winck, so gigantic in comparison, and to me she was an unresponsive little creature into whose mind I could not penetrate. She could not master the coordination required to climb stairs; she was not house-trained; and most remarkably for a whippet, she showed no inclination to run.

I disliked her name. At the Mayhew they had dubbed her Angel – and why not, with Christmas coming – but it was not a name to shout into the wind on Wimbledon Common. Before I saw her I had thought to call her Blue, a good single syllable for shouting, yet soft for the inevitable endearments. Imagine my dismay on finding that she was not blue at all, not even remotely hinting at it, but the colour of coffee so milky pale that she was like a ghost in the night, seeming to reflect the moon, her eyes as impenetrably black as cabochon gems of polished jet. No matter, I thought, Blue will still do – but then friends told me that it was the name of a pop band and thus not suitable; 'Call her Mimi,' they said, 'after all, her hand was, so to speak, frozen.'

She was Mimi for two days, but it was too twee a name for me and I disliked it enough to revert to Blue, but then I saw her stand on her hind legs to sniff a piece of cheese. She did this slowly, like a circus trick, unsupported by any prop on which to rest her forepaws, until she was as erect as any human, her hips almost out of joint, as narrow and skinny as a sculpture by Giacometti, whose human figures, otherworldly, ethereal, unreal, resemble stick men who have put on a little flesh. Thus it was that, immediately, she became plain Jack – and what a good name it was for the short and sharp command, and how softly I could say it when affection was demanded.

She took no time to learn this short sharp name. I did with her what I have always done with the naming of dogs – took her in my arms and said repeatedly, 'Your name is Jack,' just as I had done with Nusch, Winck, Mop and the dozen dogs before them. House-training, however, was a different matter. Though tiny even for a whippet, judged by her teeth she was a fully adult dog rather than an adolescent pup, yet at three or four (or even more) seemed too dimwitted or obstinate to understand. She responded to none of the customary tricks and treats of training, was physically too frail for any sort of brusque handling of the kind she must have had from her mother, too fearful for a raised voice, and pitifully terrified of being in the garden without me; never did she learn to use the dog flap that could have given her the freedom to come and go as she pleased. The company of other dogs outside did not reassure her – she merely cowered at the door, trembling, and then rushed back into the house, immediately emptying her bowels and bladder.

Her agoraphobia was so acute that for a month I did not

take her to the Common, and then she stayed too close at heel, her tail tucked between her legs. Nusch and Winck could rush off into the brambles, barking, but not Jack. Then, one early summer evening, she barked at a fox in the garden, the first sound that she had made since the early days with me when she emitted what I took to be low groans of pain. The bark was surprisingly deep and resonant for so small a dog, and oddly human too, resembling Callas at the very bottom of her register. This marked the end of her inhibitions. Six months with me and she had become a very different dog. Still skeletal, still frail, she had discovered stairs as a source of fun – though her early attempts at them were, with her long legs, uncoordinated and calamitous – and her fearful response to the garden had become one of twenty-yard dashes in a straight line as though testing her acceleration; watching her response to smells – of heron, magpie, pigeon, fox – was to observe the awakening of instinct. Full of this new self-assurance, she became pushy, barking at the doorbell, shouldering old Nusch aside, plunging with Winck into dense undergrowth, though never far, never letting me out of her sight. At last I mattered to her; she waited for hours in the window and then, in a frenzy of welcome, raced to greet me with her eyeless and earless teddy bear. But on the open meadows of the Common, still she did not run.

Once up to her proper weight and hard of muscle, she was much given to squirming vigorously on her back. At night she seemed to want to sleep alone and I constructed a box with an entrance into which only she could squeeze, but after a month or two of this craving for the aedicula (the human phenomenon is the child craving for the Wendy house or security under the kitchen table), she took to emerging from it at three or four in the morning to throw herself on the floor and thrash about in an ecstasy of wriggling, and then, assuming me to have slept through this racket, sprang onto my bed to nestle behind my knees, under my chin or round my head like a living nightcap. But she did not stay still and sometimes I found myself poked and prodded by all four paws at once at the ends of rigidly extended legs, until I made more room for her; of this the consequence was that I often slept in appallingly contorted positions and woke with aching neck and creaking back. No one who has not slept with a whippet is likely to believe what an unfair amount of room in the bed so small an animal takes. Winck, I observe in passing, slept either at my feet, or with her head on the neighbouring pillow, and Nusch used to clamber into my bed for a little tummy-tickling only ten minutes or so before I dragged myself out of it in the morning.

After a full year Jack had become a normal dog, funny, affectionate, responsive and full of character. With new hair fully grown on the paws and tail that she had gnawed bare in her abandonment, she was well-nigh perfect, with a little blaze of white on her chest and a faint hint of blue in her ears and running down her spine. Curious and confident, she consumed nuts and chocolate (neither of them good for dogs), cheese and yoghurt, and all the temptations sweet and salt for which dogs sell their souls, her appetite for bananas quite insatiable. To my great pleasure she learned to break all the rules of etiquette and nothing pleased me more than her standing with trembling forepaws on the table, shaking it, insistently demanding some titbit from my plate, discreetly nipping me if I ignored her. With those same paws she pulled the duvet from my shoulders in the middle of a winter's night, and when, in the morning, I made my bed, she watched, and as soon as the covers were smooth and straight, rolled on it, mad as a maenad, an ecstatic, stretching, wriggling wildness informing spine and limb, the back arching, head and neck thrashing from side to side, and then she'd haul the cover back and make a bird's nest of my pillows.

Lord knows who had had her from a pup, who crushed her instincts and emotions, who left her to die without food and water when, like every other dog, all that she needed was a little love and understanding, a little laughter and a sense of fun. When I found all three dogs on my bed during the day, Jack nestled in the curve of Winck's belly, her head resting on Nusch's thigh, I saw what William Hogarth, the eighteenth-century painter with a pug, maintained that every man's immediate society should be 'a self-regulating community of equals'. Well, almost – I was top dog, of course, but perhaps only because I had the bank account.

This triumvirate ended with Nusch's death in November 2007. Then Jack took sole command of the old leather chair in my study and snoozed away the days, often twitching in a dream, sometimes steadily watching me. I'd swear that she could will me to break my train of thought, abandon Raphael and Picasso, and get up to talk to her, offer the endearment 'Little One', stroke her ears and run my fingers along her spine. When Lottie arrived and Jack had again to share this chair, primacy had always to be Jack's and, if denied her, with scratching claws she knew exactly how to tell me that I must correct the order of occupation, which had to be Jack in its sunken depths, with Lottie almost smothering her.

From Hecate I had learned that whippets are not like other dogs. Remarkable for her fastidiousness, Hecate hated mud on paws or belly, wiped her face vigorously after every meal (usually on Titian's beloved, the yellow velvet sofa), showed no interest in the droppings of other animals and, when dropping her own, demanded catlike privacy. Jack too disliked mud, puddles and the rain, but her fastidiousness ended with the turd (another honest English word of great antiquity that I would like to see and hear restored to polite use in place of Latin euphemisms), for these were for her what gossip columns are for me. The best of all turds were those left by a badger and I had to learn the body language that betrayed them, so unwilling was I to suffer the consequences of their discovery. She had for some weeks been on a short leash while recovering from a twisted spine, the result of a collision at speed with another dog. At last, well enough to be let loose, we returned to the Common; within seconds she disappeared into the wild wood, and in only a few seconds more, returned, I swear with a grin, having found and rolled on a badger's turd, the volume substantial, the vintage and texture perfect for her purpose – which was to smear as much of it as she could over as wide a reach of her body as possible.

She who moments earlier had been demure enough to take tea in Fortnum's had masked her cheeks and almost plugged her ears with the pungent dark brown stuff, had forced it over and under her collar and down her neck, had smeared it onto her shoulders and flanks, the vile sweetness of the smell mysterious and overwhelming. At home it seemed easily to sponge away, but the smell remained, clinging to her and everything in any room she chose to occupy. And it also stayed on me. The following day, showers and shaves later, in the middle of lecturing on the Sienese exhibition at the National Gallery, my nose itched, and in brushing the itch away I was suddenly and disconcertingly aware that on my fingertips the stink of badger's turd still lingered – an intellectual disruption so acute that for some seconds Giovanni di Benvenuto became Benvenuto di Giovanni (though I doubt if my audience could tell). On Jack herself the bouquet lasted for a week. Perhaps, as with the civet cat, some wondrous fixative for perfumes lies undiscovered in the badger's anal glands.

But still Jack did not run. Her chosen place was always close at heel and, if occasionally she followed Winck into the undergrowth, she was never out of sight and, overcome by caution, always suddenly turned tail and scampered back. When Lottie came and she and Winck raced for sticks and balls, Jack just stood still. And then, one day in her fourth summer with me, in 2008, she joined in, not racing them, but asking for a stick of her own. I threw it and she ran – and ran, and ran – in ever-lengthening bounds and widening circles until out of breath. It was as though, in discovering her ancient heritage and purpose as a running hunting dog, some instinctive joy had been released, and the game became our ritual. But I feared for her fragility and never let her enter into rivalry with Lottie; when she stood against the light I could still see something of the intricate structure of her frail and slender bones as clearly as the framework in one of Leonardo's anatomical studies, and I constantly reminded myself of the calamity of her collision with another dog. And then, in the autumn, I had to fear no longer, for she simply would not run. She stopped as abruptly as she had begun.

I soon became worryingly aware that she was slowing down, sleeping much more and needing to empty her bladder in the night. Her vet, Roger Bralow, diagnosed problems with her heart and kidneys and, in February 2009, opined that she had only months to go. In spite of pills administered in scrambled egg, her decline accelerated and evidence of cancer too became apparent. I knew that soon the cancer would cause pain, knew what would have to be done to end it, but, remembering Nusch's scream as the needle went into her vein, I wanted to put Jack down myself and asked for lethal tablets. These do not exist, but if they do, they are not to be had by ordinary mortals.

I cannot understand why no lethal sedative is available to the loving master of a dying dog. I can think of no greater gesture of affection for any animal than to see that it has a comfortable death at home, in the hands of those in whom it placed its trust.

I loved Jack, my Little One. I wanted her to live with her small pleasures to the last moment free of pain, and then to let sleep in my arms gently turn to death. I wanted her death to be serene, without the alarm and commotion of strangers in the room, but it was not quite to be. On 21 July 2009, death came to her on my lap and in my arms, and free of pain I'm sure, but Jack was aware of strangers and disturbance, and our parting was not as it should have been, just for us, alone.

≈ 13 ≈

Lottie and Gretel

Lottie is a Staffordshire bull terrier crossed with something rather longer-legged, brindle with dissonant white patches, the very image of a dog in a painting by Stomer, a deaf and dumb Dutchman of the early seventeenth century. Her head is disproportionately large, her profile far from noble, and full-face she has something of the monkfish in her looks, not helped by an eye that wanders far further to the right than God intended. To perfection for a week or so she played the hangdog role of the cowed and beaten cur, the rejected mutt, the tyke abandoned and reviled, belying her weight, volume and hard muscle – the flesh beneath her silken coat has as little give in it as marble. I suspected that her first owner had tried to make her the fashionable aggressive weapon-dog favoured by hoodies and members of far right fascist parties (and with her black leather studded collar she almost looked the part), but managed only to cow the spirit and affection that my indulgent company was to release.

She was sick on the way home on the grey and chilly afternoon of 8 March 2008. Almost certainly a stranger to cars, she seemed to think mine a trap and was in evident distress the moment she got into it, even though Winck had clambered in readily enough to reassure her. Worse for her, perhaps, she was in it with two men – for I was soon to learn that though she felt no fear of women, her reaction to men was very close to terror; even now, five years later, she is embarrassingly wary of any man coming to the house, retreating yet lurking with baleful bloodshot eyes, springing away from any hand reached out. That she bore no wounds when, some weeks earlier, her owner left her tied to the railings of the Mayhew Home overnight with only an unopened tin of dog food for company, indicated that she could not have been used as training bait for a fighting dog, but I had never known another dog so scared of men and could only assume that she had frequently been beaten. She was so fearful that it was only with much patience that I was eventually allowed to fondle her, and years later, even to men she knows she never warms.

When we reached home Jack took one look at her and disappeared in a profound sulk, while Lottie, recovered from her nausea, raced about the garden like a mad thing – though whether through joy at her freedom or in desperation to escape I could not tell – at one point crashing into a treasured antique terracotta flower pot so large and heavy that it took two men to move, leaving it in fragments, the ancient sage bush planted in it by my mother half a century before, uprooted, never to recover. This lunatic activity ended only when she plunged into the pond, the deep end, eight feet deep.

The staff of the Mayhew estimated her age as approaching two, but I thought her much younger – only a year or so. In the house it was immediately clear that she had not been trained and I had to marshal the traditional resources of soda water, newspaper and patience, but it did not take long to civilise her, for Winck played a useful part in this, demonstrating the use of the dog flap; having an instinctively well-mannered older dog to set example makes house-training infinitely easier. Other matters took a little longer:

standing on her hind legs she pawed butter from the table and a whole roast chicken disappeared leaving only the empty dish to tell the tale. In first raiding the steel waste-bin in the kitchen she got her head and shoulders stuck in it, and in her panic made noise enough to wake the dead; then she discovered that the lid of the bin could be raised by the slightest pressure of a paw and, in succession, I found her munching an egg-box, a very stale head of broccoli and the carcass bones of a chicken. Then she gnawed old Nusch's basket and, exactly as Winck had done a decade earlier, stole my glasses, crumpled the steel frame and scarred the lenses. 'Take her back to the dogs' home,' said friends, thinking her unsuitably laddish and loutish. 'Never,' said I. 'Never.'

Once accustomed to walking on the Common, if frustrated by any delay in setting off for it, she scrabbled the hall carpets into a heap if the front door was closed, and dragged them into the garden if it was open. Once there and off the lead I discovered that, like Titian before her, she could disappear for many minutes, never responding to my despairing shouts (I grateful only that I had not, as I briefly considered, named her Schadenfreude), and eventually reappearing far ahead or to one side, but never from the direction in which she had first run. I think she runs in ever-increasing circles until she can no longer hear my cries, and then forges a direct radial line back to me – I know that she is constantly on the run because she is always breathless. Her idea of swimming in the Common ponds was, and is still, to rush into the water and paddle furiously with her forepaws while keeping her hind paws on the bottom until she is almost vertical and out of her depth, and then panic.

A passer-by on the Common once observed that Lottie has wonderful teeth for grinding table legs; this she has never done and has grown beyond that stage, but wrecking my bed and tumbling the standard lamps (the shades of which remain bent in weird distortions), were pastimes on which Winck cast a jaundiced eye and from which Jack fled, too fragile for such japes. She learned not to steal their food, nor mine, though she has an opportunist approach to anything held in the hand too long – a whole peach, for example, snatched and swallowed in a gulp. In the garden she continues to enjoy biting twigs off shrubs and has reduced many to uncomely leafless stumps.

All this I have taken in my stride, discerning no real fault or vice in her, only the virtues of a loving faithful dog – her only flaw a tendency to break wind far too often, silently and insidiously, the emanation sometimes so mephitic in my bedroom as to wake me from deep sleep.

Lottie eventually settled down to snooze with Jack in the hours between these bouts of chaos, cuddled close and intertwined, and was even a little motherly (whippets always crave the warmth of other beings). When Jack died, Lottie, clearly grieving, abandoned the old leather chair they shared and left it empty so that to me it was a bleak reminder of our loss. Often I found her sitting on Jack's tomb, staring into space, but at the same time she tried to become something of the lapdog that Jack used to be, funny and foolish, absurdly affectionate, but much too large for that. Even heavier now, at six or so her shoulders broad but her hips still slim, she is a mass of hard uncuddly muscle, her leaping prodigious though not quite the seven feet of garden wall that she could clear when she first came, her running so immediately accelerative that I'd swear her to be faster off the mark to twenty miles an hour than any Lamborghini and able to trounce all Olympic athletes over one hundred metres. Throw a ball and she explodes into the chase, but, boss-eyed as she is, she has difficulty following its path after the first wayward bounce, for the skewed right eye is the one she uses on the straight fast run and thus is blind to any ball that bounces to her left. Then she must quarter the ground and plunge into the undergrowth until, with nose rather than eye, she finds it – I am fascinated by this canine reasoning.

She smothers me with demonstrations of affection, some of which begin with her hurling herself at me at hip or shoulder height, and I have learned that I must either sidestep or stand against some stout support if I am to parry or catch her exocet approaches, rather than be felled, as I have been, so far giggling helplessly but, nevertheless, aware that some damage might be done. When not flying through the air, she stands erect on her hind legs and, like a toddling child, clings to my thigh with what I now see as her arms, her forepaws, as near as dammit, used as hands.

I thought the adolescence of this wilful and very physical bitch would never end; as a young adult she was still as warm, playful and trusting as a puppy, but too much boisterousness can become wearying for an old man whose reserves of energy, unlike Lottie's, are not inexhaustible. But end the adolescence did, with the coming of Gretel in September 2010. Gretel, a shaggy-coated border terrier with a surprised expression that I can only interpret as 'How can you be so silly?' is not my dog; she belongs to the friend who has, in my dotage, slowly and subtly assumed many of the duties of my dog ownership, leaving me with the comfortable delusion that I am still wholly responsible for them. I am not; I am an old fool on crutches with a crumbling spine and a heart that is as disorderly as a single-cylinder diesel engine of much the same age. It was he who found Gretel, the runt of a litter, six weeks old and far too young to leave her mother, small enough to settle in my cupped hands, smaller even than Penny as a puppy, sixty-five years before. A nursing job, I thought, and so too did Lottie who, apart from my providing food and drink, became the gentlest and most long-suffering of surrogate mothers.

It was extraordinary to see this hard-muscled obstreperous hound become, immediately, so gentle and considerate. Lottie kept her clean and educated her in careful and indulgent play, letting the pup sink her teeth, pinprick sharp, into her wagging tail in her attempts to still it or even chew it raw. She lay recumbent and Gretel clambered about her silken slippery slopes as though climbing Mount Ararat. Lottie taught her to run and chase and tease and wrestle, and never lost her gentle touch. Now that both are adults, they still play, but not so much, for Gretel's terrier nature cannot be denied and she has other things to do. Fearless, she must see off the foxes, squirrels, magpies, wood pigeons and other intruders in whom Lottie is no longer interested, and has become the garden's guardian; she has also become a devotee of David Attenborough's television programmes and defends me from lion, elephant and ape. Lottie looks after the house, a watchful, baleful presence in the window, her hearing so acute that from the peculiar timbre of a single bark I know of visitors before they ring the bell in the garden wall.

This chapter I must leave unfinished – Lottie and Gretel will surely see me out.

Coda

That men should live with dogs in today's society is no longer a reasonable proposition – nor has it been since we ceased to be hunter-gatherers and instead settled in cities. As Charles Pooter, suburbanite extraordinary, might have observed had George and Weedon Grossmith not cut short his *Diary of a Nobody* in 1892, a dog contributes nothing to the household income, pays no taxes, plays no role in church or state, stands no rounds in pubs and clubs, and is wholly dependent on the charity of mankind for bed and board.

What does he offer in return? Constant demands for food – his own, which he does not share, and yours, of which he expects to be given the really tasty bits; he shakes his wet coat next to your bookshelves and ruins the precious dust jackets of your rare editions; he clambers onto your bed and leaves it damp and muddy, or into it, depositing earth and sand that make your sheets as gritty as a Sussex beach; he may, if territorially inclined, leave little squirts of urine on the legs of every chair and table in the house, and on every trailing curtain and bed cover, costing you a small fortune in soda water. His loose hair he leaves on your furniture and clothes, and your house is full of bachelors' rabbits, those balls of fluff that only emerge from under the bed when visitors arrive to stay; and of his passionate sexual assaults on the swinging foot of any friend unwise enough to cross his legs, the least said, the better.

No sane Mr Pooter, respectable resident of Holloway,

would dream of having such an irrelevant monster in his tidy house. I, on the other hand, not the least bit Pooterish, lacking boot scraper, housemaid, wife and family, am more than content to have, not just a dog, but dogs about me. Dogs are utterly unselfish, though perhaps occasionally thoughtless, and will surrender their little souls for you if that is what you want. A dog's devotion is unquestioning, undemanding and undiminishing; he never cares how you look first thing in the morning, does not look aghast at belch or fart, nor does he grumble if you choose not to shave. He doesn't care a damn whether you drive the latest Mercedes-Benz or a clapped-out Morris Minor, for he has no vanity. He responds to your foulest mood by minding his own business and asks nothing of you more than food and water, a daily walk or two, and physical gestures of affection. He laments your going and rejoices at your coming back.

The dog even offers considerable advantages over the wife, the mistress, the toy-boy and the paramour: you do not have to take him out to lunch or dinner, conspire to be away for long weekends, share a bank account with him or settle outrageous bills run up on credit cards. You do not have to remember your dog's birthday, proposal day, wedding day or any other anniversary; and you do not have to mend your quarrels with perfume and red roses, because you never quarrel with a dog.

By all means let the Mr Pooters of this world hold the view that no sane man would share his life with such an animal – but if living without the lunatic companionship of dogs is proof of sanity, please God, let me be mad.

Penny, walking from Penshurst to Knole, 22 July 1946

Above: Susie with two
pups in the garden at
Castle Hedingham,
1964

Middle: Susie in my
bedroom, the day
before her death in
1975

Below:
Ginny crowded by
her pups, Spinoza and
Gamage nearest,
Autumn 1970

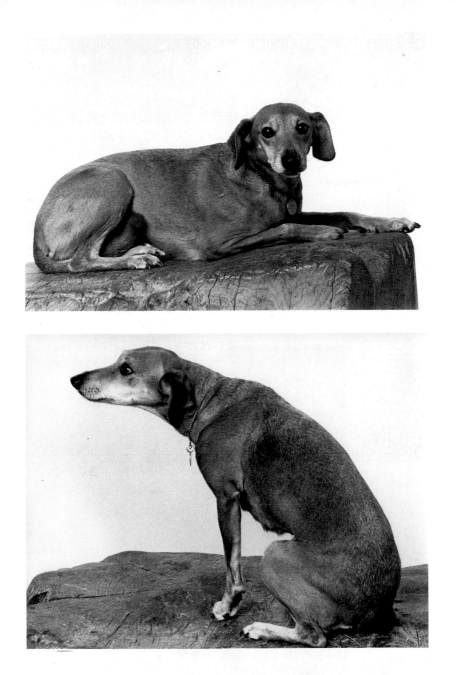

Top and Bottom: Ginny, having recovered her figure after pregnancy, posing for John Vere Brown, December 1970

Top: Hecate halfway down the steps of the house
in Eldon Road, Summer 1973

Bottom: Schubert, Summer 1973

Trollop after her discovery of Catkin and her kittens in July 1978

Trollop, already wet, below a BATHING PROHIBITED
notice at the Serpentine

Top: Trollop begging for ice cream

Bottom: Gamage leaping into the Serpentine,
Schubert just ahead of her in the splash

Schubert and Gamage leaping for a stick, Trollop barking,
Hecate just visible behind Trollop

Spinoza in extreme old age, the last of the line,
at the Serpentine Gallery, December 1986

Top: Mrs Macbeth through the railings round the changing
rooms of swimmers in the Serpentine

Bottom left: Titian on the steps of the house in Eldon Road
Bottom right: Catkin looking through the garden wall in Eldon Road

Top: Mop with Titian on their settee in the kitchen, Titian's whiskers white with age, Summer 1994

Bottom: Mop with me after Titian's death and my first heart attack

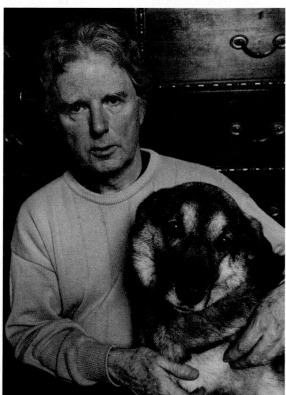

Top: Nusch rolling –
as on the dead fish

Bottom;
Early morning in
Kensington Gardens
with Mop and Nusch,
February 1999

Winck in the Wimbledon garden, June 2003

Winck, Summer 2012, partly recovered from her stroke

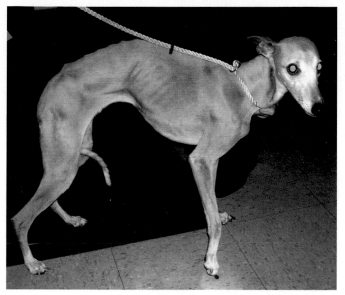

Top: Jack, cowed and emaciated, as collected
from the Mayhew Home in 2005

Bottom: Jack recovered, mischievous

Above: Lottie, Jack and Winck, Summer 2008

Below: Lottie sitting on the DOMINICANES sarcophagus
in which lie the remains of Jack and Winck